Introduction.

We have all asked ourselves the question 'Why?'. From the age of six, I have asked myself that same question almost every single day and night of my life. This book is a true and honest account of my life from a young age, showing how vulnerable some children are and how they are exploited. I have had a closed box inside my head for over 30 years, containing the horrors of my early and teenage years at the hands of an abusive alcoholic stepfather. I have chosen to put my story on paper to try and clear that box out and throw that box away, leaving it all in the past. What you are about to read you might find upsetting and disturbing, but this is what some children are going through right now. Hopefully my story helps someone going through it to find the strength and courage to go for help.
I have changed names and place for legal and protection reasons.

"Why"

Chapter one

My life was rocky right from the start. I start my story over 30 years ago back in the early Eighties, in Basildon, Essex.

My dad had left my mum when I was around the age of two but now I know what my mum put him through as family and friends have told me. I don't blame him as he couldn't do anything without being accused of cheating.

He wasn't even allowed to look at a newspaper because of page three-everyone has a breaking point and he left. It was the same with the second marriage of two to three years to John. During this marriage my big brother Chris was taken into care and I wouldn't see him again for many years.

After the break down of the marriage to John, my mum tried to take her own life with an overdose. This meant me and my big sister Katie were sent round the corner to live with my dad's sister Dot. We stayed with her for about six weeks, until mum was well enough for us to return home to ford road. If I had known then what I know now, I would've run as fast as I could and never looked back. My mum was still low and hurting when we returned home, but I was back.

"Why"

My mum and Katie started to settle into life again. A
few months had passed mum found herself a little job.
Sometimes mum would take me and Katie to work with
her. She worked voluntary, in a Cafe in the centre of
town. It was a long wooden hut with a few tables and
chairs, on one side there was an old pool table. The air
was always thick with cigarette smoke and the same
people were always there. The bit that interested me
was the toys in the corner, that I could play with all the
time I was there. It was nice that things where slowly
getting back to normal and nothing seemed different...
Until one day we was at the cafe with mum; she had
taken a big man with pictures on his arms a cup of tea.
She sat down opposite at the table; they were laughing
and chatting they looked funny together as mum being
short and chubby and him tall and bulky.
 Mum called me over and said, 'Say hello to Alan.'
He said 'Hello' and smiled at me but he smelt funny.
 I went back to the toys, leaving them laughing and
chatting again. Mum was smiling which she hadn't done
in a long time. I was happy to see her smile again as I
loved my mum and I wanted her to be happy. I was
six , the youngest of my mum's three children. Soon
Alan started coming round to our house having dinner
with us; sometimes he would stay over night, which
soon became a regular thing. After a short while and, as
usual, my mum jumped in feet first. Within a few
months of knowing Alan, he had moved in with us.

"Why"

In Another few months they told everyone they were getting married. I was really happy for mum as Alan treated my mum well and she seemed to be back to her old self again. This was good because I was always worrying about my mum being OK. Mum and Alan set about planning their wedding. They booked a registry office and mum bought a cream dress from a charity shop. On the day of the wedding me and Katie had matching dresses. We all arrived in a taxi at the registry office together. Standing outside the registry office was mum's friend Julie and her husband. We all went into a big room inside which was empty apart from us.

After they was married we went back to our house. Mum had laid on a small spread with a wedding cake; Our neighbours popped in for a while.

The lady from next door asked mum, 'When are yours and Alan's families getting here?'

Mum replied 'They can't make it-they are all busy.'

Mum seemed like she was happy at this stage. I was happy about life as well, because I was thinking of something big that was going to happen to me. I was starting at William ford infant school very soon. We weren't a rich family but I was excited . On my first day I was standing in front of mum, in my new blue school uniform and shiny black shoes. Mum plaited my hair, with a pretty ribbon which was bright pink-my favourite colour. I skipped all the way to school which was only a few minutes walk away from my house.

"Why"

It was a big building with big blue gates and a clock on the roof. There were hundreds of other children, with their mums waiting in the playground in front of the school. Mum stayed with me until the bell rang. A teacher was standing at the door calling out names of children; one by one they all made a line next to her then I heard her call my name. I said, 'Bye mum,' And joined the back of the line. The teacher said, 'Right we are all here, lets go to our classroom.' As soon as I walked in the building my excitement turned to fear. I was sat in a classroom with about 25 other children. There was tables with our names on them which had four chairs each table. Mrs Potts said, ' Find your name and sit down.'

I was sitting at a table with two boys and a girl;we all had to stand up in turn and say hello and tell the class our names. The other girl at my table was Sally-she had her hair up in pig tails and she had the same colour ribbon in her hair, which is how we started talking. I loved Mrs Potts our teacher-she was very well spoken, with a soft voice and a very friendly face.

 Me and my brand new friend hit it off. If I am honest my first real friend, because my mum never liked us to play out. At playtime, me and sally went out into the massive playground at the back of the school with all the other schoolchildren. We played hide and seek, we ate our lunch together; basically right from the start we were by each other side at school.

"Why"

That first day at school was better than I thought it was going to be. After a full day at school I was getting tired when mum come to get me. I didn't skip home I was too tired, I was talking all the way home, Telling my mum about my brand new friend Sally, and all about my lovely teacher and my wonderful day and that all my fears had disappeared, as I had my new friend sally. Life was pretty much normal at this time of my life. I loved school; I had hot dinners at school because you got them free.

I didn't mind as me and sally both had them, so we could have lunch together. My favourite subject at school was art; I loved painting and drawing. When I had been at school for a few weeks, I did a painting and it was so pleased when my teacher put it up on the wall.

I hated P.E because I wasn't very good at it as when I was young I was a little chubby which made it hard to do. I was a good child at school. I was brought up to respect adults. Apart from PE school was going well for a few weeks but things were about to change.

In the same class as me and sally was a new a boy called Ben.

He started pulling my hair every time he walked passed me in the corridor.

In the school gardens there was a little fish pond; me and sally was standing looking at the fish. When Ben came running past and pushed me in. I was scared out of my wits because I couldn't swim. Luckily enough one of the dinner ladies was nearby and dragged me out.

"Why"

 I was really upset-, my nice new shoes that I had been
very careful with to keep nice and clean were wrecked,
soaking wet and thick with mud. I was taken to the
headteacher's office and really told off for being so close
to the pond as we weren't allowed anywhere near it.
After that I found out that Ben liked me- if you ask me
its a bit strange. but I suppose that's boys for you!
 If I thought the telling-off my teacher gave me was bad
and scary I was wrong.
 When my mum picked me up, I was wearing spare
clothes the school gave me and holding a letter to give to
my mum to come and speak to my teacher.
 I walked out and gave the letter to my mum, then we
went back into my classroom. As I sat there quite next to
mum the teacher told her what had happened. After the
teacher had finished, mum grabbed my hand and walked
me out of my classroom. We headed out of the school.
Mum didn't speak to me all the way home. When we
reached home, mum opened the door. We walked in and
mum slammed the front door behind me. Then I felt this
pain-I'd never felt anything like it before. Mum belted
me really hard round the head.
My ears rang; I started to cry and mum told me to go
straight to my room and shouted that she hadn't finished
with me yet. I didn't know what this meant, but I soon
found out I went upstairs and did as I was told. When I
reached my room I lay on my bed and held my head in
my hands because it was hurting so much.

"Why"

 I could hear raised voices from downstairs, followed by
heavy footsteps on the stairs. Then the door of my
bedroom flew open and there was Alan standing there
with a leather belt in his hand. What happened next was
terrifying. He told me to get up and bend over my bed.
I did what I was told like I always did. He pulled my
skirt up and my knickers down 'This is for wrecking
your shoes,' he shouted.
 He then grabbed the top of my arm tightly, hitting me
really hard with all his strength four times with his belt
across my bum.
It felt like my bottom was bleeding after the beating he
had dished out. When he let go of my arm he stormed
out of my room. I couldn't sit on my bed, I was in too
much pain. I didn't get anything dinner that night either.
I was just sent to bed. I didn't care-I was hurting too
much to think about being hungry and I cried myself to
sleep that night.
  The following morning I sheepishly went downstairs
to have my breakfast. Katie was already up; she was
sitting at the dining table eating her breakfast. I sat down
next to her with a wince as my bottom still tender and
stinging from last nights beating. Katie was three years
older than me and she wasn't as chubby as me. I took
after my mum and she must've taken after my dad; she
had jet black hair- my hair was mousey brown. we did
get on but we weren't close; we would fight all the time.
On that morning she loved pointing out that I was in
mum's bad books.

"Why"

I saw my lovely new shoes near the back door, still all muddy but they had dried. Then I heard someone coming down the stairs; it was Alan. He came in to the kitchen without a word to make himself a cup of tea. He looked at me like I was dirt; something seemed to have changed.

He eventually grunted at me. 'Clean your shoes and be ready before your mum comes down to take you to school.'

I did as I was told. I had to go out in the garden and clean the mud from my shoes.

It was late October and it was freezing outside. So I cleaned them as quickly as I could. If I thought the weather was frosty it was nothing compared to the treatment that my mother gave me- she looked and spoke to me like I was dirt.

She was downstairs when I went back into the house. I kept my head down and got ready for school. I waited for mum to take me- what a relief when we arrived at school.

Mum left me at the school gates; she just turned and walked away without saying a word.

I spotted my friend sally; everything was nice and happy again. Ben, the boy that had pushed me into the pond, was made to say sorry. It didn't make any difference from there on. he picked on me without getting caught. He still pulled my hair and called me names. Now I was wearing my shoes that had lost their shine he called me a scank.

"Why"

I tried to take no notice but it made me sad. I tried to stay away from him and most of the time I managed it. Ben had started to make my school days hell; he asked sally if I would be his girlfriend. I was shocked but happy because he was really cute. So from that day my school days where happy again but home life was getting worse.

"Why"

Chapter two

I was happy at school, Christmas was fast approaching. There was a massive Christmas tree in the school hall; each class had taken it in turns to decorate. We was all busy make Christmas cards for our mum's and making decorations to hang on our trees at home.
The nearer Christmas got the more excited I became.
But like I said home life was changing and not in a good way.
It had now become the norm, that mum and Alan was treating me and Katie like slaves. When we got in from school, we had chores to do like hoovering and the washing up after mum and Alan had finished their dinners. Me and Katie was only allowed a sandwich when we got in from school. We was told as we had hot dinners at school we didn't need another one.
It wasn't just the housework we had to do- we were treated like kids should not be seen or heard.
We had to spent most of our time at home in our bedrooms. We were Mostly allowed downstairs when they wanted a cup of tea made.
We was allowed to watch TV sometimes but it was very rare and it was only what they were watching.
Mum never took me and never came to pick me up from school anymore.

"Why"

Mum told me, 'You have to pretend that you are going out of the school gates with one of the other mum's.' This was fine with me: most of the time it was sally's mum that walked me to the top of ford road.

My excuse was either my mum was busy working or wasn't very well.

One day when I got home Alan wasn't in. Mum had a horrible looking bruise of all nasty colours under one of her eyes.

I asked, 'Are you OK?'

Mum answered, ' Mind your own business and get on with your chores.'

While doing my chores, I noticed that the stereo had gone from the front room as well.

I didn't say anything to mum about it; I didn't dare to as the mood she was in.

So I finished my chores and went to my room to keep out of the way.

Katie was already finished and lying on her bed in her room; it was about half seven.

Mum shouted up the stairs at me and Katie, 'You two can turn off your lights and go to sleep.'

I put the drawing which id been doing on the pile of drawings next to my bed and lay in my bed to settle for the night.

By this time Alan was still not home. I didn't care because mum had left me alone. I started to drift off to sleep, Suddenly I was awoken with a really loud bang. Making me jump out of my skin as I was half asleep.

"Why"

I sneaked out on to the landing as quietly as I could,
where I found Katie who had been woken up by the
noise coming from downstairs.
We could hear mum was still up, then all we could hear
was shouting and mum crying.
I know now that I was stupid. I was worried about mum
so I went down the stairs. Mum and Alan was standing
in the front room. Alan was wobbling on his feet and
finding it hard to stand up.
Then he spotted me at the door way.
Staggering in my direction, his eyes full of rage and his
face red with anger, he grabbed a handful of my hair.
Shouting at mum: 'Your little bastard needs to learn a
lesson.'
What for? why? what had I done wrong? I didn't have a
clue.
He threw me to the floor by my hair and started using
me as a football. Kicking all over my body- I really
thought he was going to snap me in half. After what
seemed like forever, he stopped laying in to me and
went into the kitchen.
He left me battered lying on the living room floor.
I took a glance between my hands that were covering
my face at mum- she was wiping the blood from her
puffy lip.
I was hurting everywhere. Somehow, I dragged my
body back towards the stairs. With all the strength I had
left I crawled back up the stairs.
When I reach the top Katie was nowhere to been seen- I
guessed she had retreated back into her room.

"Why"

Once I managed to get back into bed, I lay there looking at the bedroom door, trying to work out what had just happened and why .

My ears straining to listening for his foot step on the stairs, just in case he hadn't finished with me and was coming up to give me another hiding.

All I could hear was a lot of noise coming from downstairs; it sounded like all the plates and glasses where being smashed.

All I could really think about was my poor little six year old body, battered and bruised.

Every time I tried to get comfortable in bed, it felt like my tiny bones where broken- I had sharp reminder of the pain that my body was in.

Sleep was the only thing that eased the pain; the slightest movement and the pain would wake me up.

In the morning I was too scared to go downstairs, as I could hear Alan in the kitchen.

Luckily mum came into my room and said, 'You can have a day off school today.'

I replied 'Why? I want to play with sally.'

She snapped back, 'You just can't go Marie end of.'

I didn't know why, but now I look back it must have been all the bruising that covered my body.

I heard Katie getting ready for school and call out 'Bye' to mum as she left the house for school.

I must have drifted off to sleep, the next thing I knew was mum in my bedroom with a sandwich, saying 'you need to eat something, its lunch time.' The rest of that day passed in a blur.

"Why"

I was allowed back to school after a few days because I
had no visible bruising left. I tried my best to avoid
Alan after that night, but it was impossible as we lived
in the same house. After this incident all that made me
happy was school, seeing my best friend sally. When I
went back to school sally seemed as pleased to see me
as I was to see her.
 After a couple of days of me being back at school,
 She told me, ' My birthday is coming up and I am
allowed two friends round for tea; I want you and Ben
to come.'
With my fingers crossed: 'I will have to ask my mum if
its ok.'
 How lucky was she: a birthday tea and Christmas
getting nearer.
 I was so excited and surprised when mum let me go to
sally's house for tea. I had never been to a birthday party
before.
We where breaking up from school for the Christmas
holidays.
On the second day of the holidays, me and Ben went
round to sally's for her birthday tea. When we arrived
sally was waiting for us at the door,with her mum.
After we had played pass the parcel and music chairs we
all sat up the table, tucking into sandwiches and crisps.
When we had finished our tea, sally's mum turned off all
the lights. A second later she was walking into the dining
room, with a pink birthday cake with seven lit pink
candles, and we sang happy birthday. It was so
wonderful.

"Why"

I didn't want it to end, but sadly sally's mum said that she would walk me home.

When I got home, everyone was in the front room. Mum and Katie were decorating the Christmas tree. Alan was standing on a ladder, hanging pretty decorations on the ceiling.

Once everything was done, I put the angel I had made at school on the top of the tree.

The room looked like fairytale land; even Alan was being nice. Me being stupid, I let myself think that maybe he had changed back to the nice man I had first meet at the Cafe.

A few days went passed without one nasty word or slap, then it had finally arrived: Christmas morning.

Me and Katie raced downstairs to see if there was any presents under the tree. The morning went on with presents and everyone happy, with the smell of Christmas dinner cooking.

Mum called out 'get yourselves up the table.'

The table was decorated with a Christmas tablecloth and a Christmas cracker each.

We all sat down to a big dinner with all the trimmings. Alan was being nice and my guard was well and truly down.

But once dinner was done, Alan started to drink his beer, one can after another. That funny smell he had the first time I met him was back again.

The happy Alan had gone and the nasty Alan was back. The first sign he had changed back was, me and Katie was sitting playing with our toys.

15

"Why"

 He came over and shouted at both of us, 'I haven't
given you two permission to play with your present yet.'
Before I could grab the lovely colouring book and pens,
that father Christmas had left under our pretty Christmas
tree for me, Alan had them in his hands, screwing the
book up and snapping the pens; he threw them on the
open fire.
Then he grabbed Katie's little baby doll and did the
same with that.
As he walked away from the fire,he snatched my angel
from the tree ripping her in to pieces and threw her on
the fire.
Alan slurring his words said, 'You two sit there and
watch that lot burn.'
 All I heard over the crackling of the fire was his laugh.
My eyes welling up with tears, I remembered asking
Santa for a doll and colouring book with pens as the toys
laid on the fire burning.
 Mum come in from the kitchen, shouting at him-but not
because he had taken our toys off us but because he had
wasted her money.
 He grabbed Katie by the hair, pulling her to her feet,
slapping her round the head and pushing her towards the
door that lead to the stairs, shouting ' Get out of of my
sight.'
Then it was my turn for the same treatment .
 When I got to my room, I threw myself onto my bed,
sobbing.
All of a sudden the noise from downstairs erupted.
It was so loud; they were both shouting at each other.

"Why"

Then the banging and crashing started. I couldn't work out what the banging was.

Then I heard the front door slam- my bedroom was at the front of the house.

So, being careful not to be seen, I looked to see who had left.

There I saw Alan staggering away from the house, watching him bouncing off the hedgerows and cars until he was out of sight.

I plucked up the courage to go downstairs, the sight that greeted me was horrible.

There was mum in the middle of the front room, picking herself up off the floor, blood pouring from a gash over her eye. The Christmas tree was a smashed up heap on the floor and all decorations had been ripped down and torn to bits.

It was so sad to see; it wasn't my fairytale land any more. Mum just said, 'clean this up' and then she got up and went into the kitchen and cleaned her face.

When I was finished putting the tree back together. Mum let me have a chocolate from tree, letting me stay and watch a little TV.

Katie was asked if she wanted to come down as well, she chose to stay in her room.

Although it was nice I couldn't relax; I kept listening for the door. Alan didn't return that night.

On Boxing day me, mum and Katie went to see my auntie Dot.

I loved it at hers- she was lovely to me and Katie.

"Why"

When auntie Dot answered the door, she asked mum
'how did you get that cut above your eye?'
Mum never told her what Alan had done last night, but
instead told her 'I fell over in the garden.'
Then completely changing the subject telling Dot 'We
have run out of electric.'
Mum continued, 'Dot could you put us up until the shops
opened the next day please?.'
Dot said 'Yes of course you can stay.'
I was over the moon that we was staying at Dot's. That
night auntie Dot made us cold meat with bubble and
squeak for dinner.
We all snuggled up on the sofa, watching TV and
eating chocolates. It was getting late; I was fighting to
keep my eyes open.
Dot said 'You girls can sleep in the spare room but you
will have to share a bed, come on, I will come up and
tuck you in.'
She said to mum, ' I will grab you some blankets and a
pillow while I am up stairs- you can make yourself
comfortable on the sofa.'
That night I had the best night's sleep I had had in a
long time.
There wasn't any shouting or banging from downstairs
and I felt safe.
In the morning after breakfast we said our good byes
and left.
When we got back home and walked into the house my
heart sank. I remembered-the Christmas images came
back to me.

"Why"

Alan still hadn't returned. For four days life was as normal as it could be.

Most of my time was spent in my room, doing what I loved - drawing - then new year's eve came.

I woke and had my breakfast and then went back to my room.

I like being in there on my own. While I was sitting on my bed drawing.

I heard a key go into the front door and it opened. A chill went through my whole body, when I heard Alan's voice telling me and Katie ' come down.'

I was too scared not to go down. We went into the front room. There stood Alan, with a large box in front of him.

He said, ' Have a look in the box.'

We peaked into the box, half expecting something to jump out at us then he announced 'We was going to have fireworks later tonight- 'mum is doing some hotdogs to eat while watching the fireworks.'

I let myself get excited, Katie wasn't very happy because she was scared of fireworks.

Alan told Katie, 'You can watch them out of the kitchen window.'

All day I was thinking of fireworks. As the light started to fade Alan walked into my bed room and asked, 'Are you ready to help me with the fireworks?'

I was happy to help if it made him happy.

Mum had done the hot dogs as he had asked. We all had one each then out me and Alan went.

He said I had a really big girls job to do.

"Why"

He gave me a really long stick that had a flame on the end.

Then after a few minutes of him being at the bottom of the garden, sorting which fireworks where going to be used first, he came and got the stick from me. The fireworks were all colours. Every time he lit a firework he let me hold the stick.

Then he took the biggest firework out of the box, taking it down the bottom of then garden. He lit it and run back to me giving me the stick.

All of a sudden there was a massive boom; it made me jump out of my skin it was so loud. I dropped the stick and the flame went out.

He called to mum 'Chuck me a lighter to light this again,'

He lit the stick but didn't give it back to me; he walked down the garden with it. When he came back he had a firework in his hand, with sparks pouring from it and doing the laugh I would end up fearing.

He handed me the firework. I didn't know what to do- the heat coming off it and the sparks burning my hands - it was red hot.

He shouted, 'Drop my stick will you ? ,How dare you?, you are spoiling it for everyone.'

I was terrified. He grab it and threw it down to the bottom of garden.

He told me 'We aren't going to do any more fireworks because you are a naughty girl.'I was so scared. When I went indoors where he told me to go.

Mum said, 'Thanks for that, now his going to be really mad. Go to your room.'Sadly she was right.

"Why"

 That night he told me to come downstairs, so I went
down not knowing what he wanted me for, as it was late
and my bedtime. But I soon found out. Katie was in bed
by this time. I stood in front of him and mum.
Then he instructed me, 'Sit in the corner of the room,
face the wall cross your legs and put your hands up in
the air above your head,' adding 'If your hands touch
your head you will know all about it.'
 So there I was sitting with my arms up. I was there what
seemed like ages. My little arms started to get heavy and
ache. They was getting closer to my head and I was
finding it hard to stay awake.
 I don't know if id dozed off, when I felt this pain in the
middle of my back - something had hit me hard.
 I turned round to find his slipper laying on the floor
behind me.
He had thrown it at me and, by the feeling in my back
very hard, With mum sitting beside him he started
shouting at the top of his voice.
'Why are you are so thick? can't you do anything?'
I wanted to cry but I kept it inside - it would of made
him more angry and shout even more.
Yelling at me: 'Now fuck off to bed, you are making me
sick at the sight of you.' I just managed to get to my feet
with my back stinging.
As I bent it to get up the pain doubled. I shuffled to the
lounge door.
Glancing at mum - she hadn't taken her eyes from the
TV the whole time he had been shouting at me.

"Why"

That night sleep wouldn't come. I was confused; I didn't know why he hated me so much. I was really tired in the morning, but still had to get up and make mum and Alan a cup of tea, taking it up to them while they laid in bed. At last something good did happen that day, it was just after dinner. Me and Katie was given beans on toast and mum and Alan had chops, mash with peas.

I was in the kitchen with Katie, I was washing up and she was drying. Mum and Alan was sitting in the lounge watching TV. There was a knock at the door I heard someone open it, I heard some voices that I didn't know. Then mum called us in to the lounge, sitting on the sofa sat a lady and a man that I had never seen before. Mum said, 'This man is your dad.'

I didn't know what to do; I didn't know this man. He got up and walked over to where me and Katie was standing and asked, 'Can I have a cuddle please?'

When I got into his arms it felt perfect and loving, but I wish he hadn't squeezed me so hard as my back was still sore. I really didn't mind because I loved his cuddle.

Dad said, 'This lady with me is Mary.' she seemed really nice.

After a short while we was told to go upstairs because the adults needed to talk. Me and Katie sat at the top of the stairs trying our hardest to listen; then the voices stopped. We scrambled straight to our rooms, knowing if we got caught we would be harshly punished. I rushed to my bedroom window and watched Dad and Mary walk up the path and get into a car.

"Why"

As they drove away I thought my dad must be rich because he had a car.

After that day life settled back to normal. Christmas was gone and forgotten about but I didn't mind it wasn't a happy one for me.

A few weeks after Christmas, it was back to school which made me smile: I would get to see my friends again.

That first day was great. I got up and had some toast because mum didn't have any cereal. I got myself dressed but I was a bit sad because I still didn't have any new shoes. I put the old ones on I didn't care today, I was going to school and getting out of the house away from Alan for a while.

When I arrived in the playground, there was sally waiting for me.

We walked into to school together and sat next to each other just like before Christmas. That day was so nice, there was one activity that filled me with sadness.

Mrs Potts said that we all had to draw a picture of what we got for Christmas. I drew a picture of my colouring book and pens.

Then the memory came back to me, about how they looked burning on the fire and my fairy wonderland that was smashed to bits.

At play time sally told me that she had a great time over the Christmas. she asked, 'Did you have a nice Christmas?'

I felt really bad because I had to lie I said, 'Yes we had lots of fun.'

Chapter Three

The snow had melted away and the weather was starting to warm up. The flowers were blooming, the trees had new buds; spring was on its way. My seventh birthday was just round the corner. At breakfast shortly before my big day I asked mum, 'Can Sally and Ben come for tea on my birthday?'

She sharply replied, 'No.'

I said 'That's not fair - I went to her birthday tea.'

'I said no Marie and don't get any more ideas like that.'

I knew she was going to say no, she did let me go to sally's birthday but I wanted one of my own. I was still getting excited, hoping and praying that my birthday was going to be better than Christmas had been.

Yet again I was being stupid to even think that and only fooling myself .

It was the morning of my seventh birthday,with the sun beaming into my room. I heard mum leave the house as I lay in my bed. Mum had left me a little present on the cupboard in my room - she must have put it there when I was asleep so it was there when I woke up in the morning. I smiled when I saw it; because mum had done something nice for me on my birthday.

I ripped the wrapping paper off as fast as I could, revealing a bag of sweets and a pretty red ribbon to put in my hair. After a few minutes Alan called to me, 'Come into mine and mums bedroom.'

"Why"

 I thought he wanted his usual cup of tea and was just going to tell me to make it.

 He told me, ' Mum said you are not going to school today, you need to have a bath and wear your best smart clothes.'

So there I was home alone with Alan, which id done before but this day was going to be very different. Alan was lying in bed watching TV.

He spoke in a really friendly voice. 'Come and lay on the bed and watch TV as it's your birthday, watch some cartoons if you like.'

I did as he said as he was being nice. I sat on top of the covers and started to watch the TV. After awhile Alan said, 'You can get under the cover so you won't get cold as you only have a nightdress on.'

 I climbed in and carried on watching the cartoons.

 Once I was under the covers everything changed.
Leaning towards me Alan with his breath having that funny smell like it usual does, he said 'I am going to give you a special birthday present, but Mum doesn't have to know about because its a secret.'

Pressing his hand over my mouth, I struggled to breathe. Trying my best to wriggle free, both of my small hand on his arm, I pushed his hand away from my mouth and broke free before he punched me. The next thing I knew he was on top of me, with all the weight of his body. I couldn't move. I didn't know what was happening - why was he doing this to me. With his hand still pressing on my mouth, he started yanking at my night dress.

"Why"

Putting his hand between my legs, touching my knickers, pulling at them until he had ripped then off me.
Then I felt an excruciating burning pain and something being forced into me. I was sobbing; the more he was pushing the more excruciating the pain got.
He said, 'You can stop crying, I am giving you your special birthday present.'
He started to move around on top of me, making noises and breathing heavy. I just wanted it all to stop. Tears filling my eyes and rolling down my face, the burning pain was unbearable.
Then I felt something warm and wet on my leg and it all stopped. Releasing his hand from my mouth he rolled off me onto his back.
Fighting for my breath, trying to get off the bed, as I leaned forward I could see I was sitting in a pool of blood.
He said, 'That's great, now I've got to clean the sheets now because of you.'
He lifted his leg and brought his foot down hard on my hip. I landed with a hard thud on the floor of the bedroom. He told me to stand up and look at him. I picked myself up. He told me, ' If you ever tell your mum or anybody what had just happened, you won't see your mum ever again because I will get a big knife from the kitchen and make her bleed lots and she will die.'
He then grunted at me, 'Now go and make my morning tea.' I walked away. My whole body was shaking, my stomach feeling as if it had been ripped out. I noticed this white sticky liquid all down my legs.

"Why"

 It was like someone had sneezed on me. I went straight
to the bathroom and use toilet roll to wipe it off.
I went downstairs and made his tea. When I was carrying
his tea up the stairs, my hand was shaking so much I had
to hold the hot mug with both hands.
 He was still lying in bed and smiled at me when I
entered the room. I just looked down at my feet; I didn't
want to see his face.
  He said, 'Go and run yourself a bath because you are
dirty.'
I placed the tea on the bedside table, keeping my
distance the best I could scared he was going to grab me
again. I left the bedroom as quickly as I could and went
to the bathroom to run my bath. It was unusual: I was
going to have fresh water just for me.
 Normally we had to share the water on bath days- Alan
would use it first, then mum, then me and Katie. I
wondered why on this day, why I was allowed to have a
bath of my own. I had only had a bath two days ago, as
bath night was normally on Sunday nights. When I had
run the bath and lowered myself in. The stinging
stopped me in my tracks, as the warm water touched me
down below. There was still a burning feeling inside me.
I took a deep breath and lowered myself in slowly but it
didn't stop the stinging.
As I was trying to scrub myself clean, the door opened.
we wasn't allowed to lock the door when we was in the
bath. I tried to cover up the best I could with my tiny
hands and a flannel .

"Why"

Alan walked in and used the toilet, I thought he was
going to leave After he had finished. As he went passed
me in the bath, he grabbed my hair and pulled me down
under the water, so I was lying on my back in the bath. I
couldn't breathe. I couldn't get back up as Alan had his
big hands on me - one gripping my hair and the other
pushing down on my chest. kicking my legs I was doing
my best to get away; Once again fighting and wriggling
for my life. I needed air.
Then I was pulled up. I took a deep breath and then Alan
was on his knees next to the bath, with his face nearly
touching mine.
  He said, 'If you ever tell your mum about our secret
present then you will die as well.'
As he walked away he did that laugh, the one that gave
me chills down my spine. When he had gone, I jumped
out the bath and dried myself as quick as I could. Only
gently dabbing the towel down between my legs - it was
too painful to rub. I darted across the landing into my
bedroom and put on some of my old clothes.
 It was my birthday but I still had chores to do. I didn't
want another beating if I made my smart clothes dirty.
By the time I was dressed, Alan was downstairs and
already outside in the garden feeding his bird's and the
fish that he kept. I was glad that he was out there; he
would normally stay out there hours with them. I didn't
want to see him and I set about getting my chores done.
I had the usual washing up and hoovering to do, But
today I had to clean out the oven and wash the kitchen
floor.

"Why"

Mum never had a mop so it was on my knees with a sponge to get the job done.

Katie was at school today. I was still wondering why I had to stay home from school and why did I have to be smart.

When I finished my chores I went to my bedroom to keep out of Alan's way. I was still up there when mum got home from work.

She called me down 'You better get your smart clothes on.'

I wanted to asks why, I didn't have to in the end she told me, 'Your dad wants to take you out for your birthday.'

I rushed upstairs; I was happy but scared all at the same time. I didn't know this man that wanted to take me out, not even his name. I got my smart clothes on while I was upstairs I was thinking about what had happened that morning. I was thinking of telling my mum, but then I remembered what Alan had said.

So I thought it was better not to I loved my mum so much, I didn't want her to go away or die. I put it to the back of my mind the best I could and went downstairs to wait. Mum put my hair up in a ponytail with my new red ribbon. I was wearing a pair of jeans and my favourite pink t-shirt. I hadn't been downstairs long when there was a knock at the door.

Mum said, 'Well go and open the door, Marie.'

There standing at the door was the man had met, it was my dad.

Alan was outside again. He spent a lot of time in the garden because he smoked.

"Why"

Mum told me, 'Go and get Alan.'

I went out into the garden and told him, 'Mum wants you.'

He was standing next to the fish pond.

He said, 'Come and have a look at the fish.'

I went over to him Alan told me 'You can't tell your dad either about the present I gave you this morning, or I will have to use a knife on him as well, your dad wouldn't believe you anyway, because you are only a child and adults only believe other adults.'

I went back in to the house, with Alan following behind me. I felt Alan's hand grab my neck, his fingers on each side squeezing hard as he let out that horrible laugh.

My neck was sore but I had had worse. No one noticed that Alan had caused me pain. After he had let go he went into the lounge and shook Dad's hand.

Saying, 'Hi Barry, you alright, mate?'

Dad said 'Hello, not bad thanks.'

We all sat down. I had to sit on the floor - kids were not allowed to sit on the sofa in our house. I sat there looking at my dad. I couldn't take my eyes off him. Alan kept his eye on me too. I could feel his glare and that I was under he watchful eye. I spotted that my Dad had a big bag with him and it looked like it had a present in it. When mum had finished making Dad a cup of tea, Dad asked her, 'Can I give Marie the birthday present that I have got for her?'

Thankfully mum said, 'yes.' I was bursting with excitement when I took the present from Dad .

"Why"

 I ripped off the pink wrapping paper really quickly,
that's when I saw the beautiful doll. I loved her straight
away.

 I was trying to open the box that she was in, mum took
it off me saying, 'You can play with her later. Dad
wants to take you out.'

Mum placed her on the floor next to her chair.

I couldn't take my eyes off my new doll. Dad got up.

'You need to get your coat and shoes on, Marie.'

 Mum said, 'You will have to wear your school shoes
because they are the only ones you have.'

We walked out of the house together; he offered me his
hand but I didn't take it. I didn't know if I was allowed
to. I saw his red car I was excited. I'd not been in a car
before and I asked, 'Are we going in your car ?'

Dad said, 'Yes we are or do you want to walk instead?'

Dad opened the door, and I got in the front passenger
seat. With a stretch, I was just about tall enough to see
out of the window. Dad walked round after closing my
door and got in the driver's side and started the engine.
We were off driving down the road. I looked out of the
window wondering where we was going.

Soon I realized we was heading towards town. We
pulled into a car park. Dad drove around and around the
car park until he found a parking space. It had only been
a short ride but I still enjoyed it. We both got out of the
car.

As we walked along the high street Dad asked, 'Do you
want something to eat Marie?' I said in a quite voice,
'Yes please dad.'

"Why"

Dad said, 'Ok then we will go to the Cafe on the corner.'
We walked side by side until we reached the Cafe, going in and taking a seat by the window. The waitress come over and gave us a menu each.

Dad said, ' Have a look at the menu you can have what you want to eat.'

I didn't need to look at the menu, I knew exactly what I wanted. I asked, 'Can I have a cheese sandwich and a coke please, Dad ?'.

'Of course you can, Marie.'

When it was placed in front of me by the lady,
I said, 'Thank you.' And began to eat my sandwich.

I loved cheese but I was never allowed cheese at home, that was for adults only, so this was a real treat for me.

Dad asked, 'Do you like school?, have you got lots of friends?'

That was it, I was off, telling him all about my friends Sally and Ben. After we had finished eating my dad paid and then we left the Cafe.

When we was standing on the pavement outside the cafe, he asked me, 'What do you want to do next?' I shrugged my shoulders.

He said ' Ok lets just have a walk.' He offered his hand again, and this time I took it. He was friendly and I didn't feel scared when I was with my dad. We walked around the shops for a while.

Dad said, 'Shall we go into Tesco's and have a look upstairs?' I said,'yes dad.'

"Why"

I had been into Tesco with my mum before but I was never allowed to go upstairs to see the toys - to me it was like an Aladdin's cave up there it sold everything.
After having a good look round, I saw these nice black shoes. Before id realized Dad was standing behind me.
He said, 'Would you like them as your shoes are getting old and worn out?, mummy wouldn't mind.'
I smiled. ' yes please.'
A lady came over and asked if she could help us with anything.
Dad told her, 'I would like these shoes.'
She said to me, 'Sit down so I can measure your feet.'
Once she had measured them, she went into the back of the shop and came back with a box with a pair of shoes in. I tried them on and I was told to walk up and down the shop.
Dad said, 'Yes we will take them.'
We went to the till and Dad paid for them. I couldn't stop smiling now I had new shiny shoes. we left and went back to the car, I didn't want our time to end or to go home.
Both of us climbed into his car and again after a short drive we were back outside my house. Before I got out the car, I looked at my dad and I don't know where it came from but I said, 'I Love you and thank you for my shoes.'
He said, 'I love you too, Marie and you're welcome darling.' He walked me up to the door and knocked.
Mum opened the door, then dad said, ' I've got to go now, Marie, bye.' He left me standing with mum at the door.

"Why"

We watched him drive away again. I waited until he was out of sight and walked indoors. Bursting with excitement I started telling mum what had done with Dad. I showed mum the new shoes. Mum didn't really look at them or take any notice of me.

She Just told me, 'There is some washing up for you to do before bedtime.'

I walked into the kitchen with a heavy heart - did no one in this house love me or would just be happy for me, that id had a good birthday trip with my dad?

I put my shoes down and started to do what id been told to do. When I had finished I went into the front room.

I asked, ' Mum, where is my doll?'

She said, 'Its upstairs in your bedroom.'

I asked, 'Can I go to my room and play before bed, mum ?'

she said, 'OK.'

Off I ran upstairs; there on my bed was the box but it had been opened. I walked over and picked it up, when I pulled my new doll out of the box her head fell off. At that moment my bedroom door opened and there was Alan laughing and said 'You didn't think I was going to let you keep her, did you?'

He walked back down the stairs. I closed my door and as I held my doll in my hands crying my heart out. Why did he break my new doll ?

I went to Katie's room and asked, 'Have you got any sticky tape I can use?'

She just passed me a roll of tape, I took it back into my room and tried to fix my present. I managed to get the head to stay on but I had to be careful with her.

34

"Why"

She was still beautiful to me; she had a pretty, frilly
dress and long brown hair which I brushed but very
carefully.
That night I laid her under the covers next to me and fell
asleep while having a cuddle with my doll. When I woke
up in the morning her head had come off again. I didn't
have time to doing anything about it - I had to get ready
for school - but at least I had my lovely new shoes. I
walked to school that day feeling like a princess. when I
got there sally said, ' I like your new shoes.'
I said, 'I went out with my dad yesterday and he got
them for me.'
But I didn't tell her about the doll because It made me
sad.
Sally gave me a present too; it was a massive packet of
colouring pens, with all the colours of the rainbow and a
pad with plain paper. I left them in my desk at school,
because I didn't want to lose these ones. I had a lovely
day that day but my birthday went passed so quickly. I
hated life at home but I loved my time at school.
Home life was getting harder. One day I had dropped a
cup while washing up, and Alan went mad at me. I
coward on the floor waiting for a kick or a slap but it
never came.
He just told me, 'You can wait.'
Confused again I got up when he left and finished the
washing up. That night mum had gone to bingo with her
friend. She picked mum up and took her as she had a
car. Mum always went to bingo on Monday nights and
left us with him. I was in my room and I heard shouting
so I went nearer the door to listen.

"Why"

It was Alan in Katie's room; she was shouting back at him. I was scared for her, because of the love I felt for her. I was worried he was going to hurt Katie, so I went to her room.

He looked at me in the door way and said to Katie, 'Why can't you be like Marie?, you are too skinny and ugly, not like Marie.' He pointed my way.

I was shocked he had always told me I was dirty, now he was saying that I was better than Katie. I don't know what they were shouting about but Katie was a very hot headed girl and she got a good few slaps for it on many occasions. I don't know why I did it. Alan went to grab her and pull her to the floor. Before he could kick her, I got in the way and took the hard kicks that was coming her way - believe me it hurt.

I was happy that Katie was OK. When he was done with kicking me he went downstairs. I got up and went to my room. Katie never came to make sure I was all right. I got ready for bed, yet again hurting from a beating. That was the night he realised how he could control me.

"Why"

Chapter Four

One morning I had got myself ready for school. As I walked out my bedroom. I took a look in the direction of mum's room to see if they were up. Their bedroom door was wide open, Alan was at the window with the curtain pulled right back.

I was going down the stairs to get my breakfast,When Alan came running pass me. He nearly knocked me flying down the stairs while making a bee line to the front door. As he got to the door a letter was pushed through the letterbox by the postman. Mum came from the lounge to see who was running down the stairs. She saw Alan was about to open the letter, and went to snatch the letter he was holding. Then all hell broke loose. They both went into the lounge and started shouting at each other. I froze and sat on the stairs not wanting to go anywhere near the shouting.

Mum screaming, 'You can't take all the fucking money to go down the fucking pub drinking, we all need to eat.' Alan exploded. 'Its my name on the giro, so its all my money to do what I like with.'

I could hear that mum was crying by the sound of her voice.

'Well you went to the fucking social and claimed for me and the girls Alan, so some of that money is mine.'

"Why"

'No its fucking not you will have to find some fucking
money of your own, Sue if you want to eat; this is all
mine.'
'How can I do that? I don't get paid for working at the
Cafe and all the social money is in your name Alan.'
'That's your problem, Sue, not mine.'
'Right I'm going down the social today and putting a
claim in for just me and the girls so we get our own
money.'
'No your fucking not messing about with my money.'
There was a lot of smashing and crashing, just like at
Christmas.
Mum was screaming, 'Stop it, Alan,just fucking stop it.'
After a while it all stopped. Alan came out of the lounge
with the letter in his hand, his face red with rage
grabbing his jacket from the banister.
 He opened the front door and went out, slamming the
door behind him, nearly breaking the glass. I carried on
down the stairs and into the lounge. Mum was sitting on
the sofa. She had puffy lips and blood running from the
corner of her mouth, her eye was starting to close and
bruise appearing on her face.
 The stuff that was normally on the shelf was scattered
all over the floor. The bird cage was laying on the floor,
the two budgies inside flapping about in a panic.
'Are you ok mum?'
'Just get your breakfast Marie, and go to school.'
 So I just went into the kitchen and made some toast.
while sitting there I could hear my mum sobbing. I
finished my breakfast then I left for school.

"Why"

All day long I couldn't stop thinking of mum, our house all smashed up and why was Alan always doing this to us?

When I got home from school Alan was still not home. All evening I was jumping because I didn't know when he was coming back. He hadn't returned before I went to bed. I soon knew when he was home because there was the sound of breaking glass.

Mum shouting at him, 'Go away, you have only come home because you have run out of money.'

'Just let me in Sue.'

'No your so drunk, you can hardly stand up.'

'If you don't let me in I am going to kick this fucking door in.'

Before mum said anything he was kicking the door, bang the door open and hit the wall. He came stomping up the stairs.

Shouting, ' Its your fault, Sue,we have no money because of your little bastard's eat too much, maybe one of them can go because the money isn't enough for four people.' Mum shouted back, 'If you didn't spend it all in the pub on drink then there would be enough money.' I heard him run back down the stairs.

Mum screaming 'Help, help me.'

I know I shouldn't of but I went down - she's my mum and she needed help.

I ran down the stairs: the front door wide open with the glass smashed.

The wood hanging off the door frame where he had kicked it in. I tried to close it but it wouldn't stay shut. Alan and mum were in the lounge.

"Why"

Alan had mum up against the wall, with his hands round her the throat, her face bright red. He dropped her to the floor as soon as he saw me.

I thought he was going to turn on me.

Staring at me he put some of his rock music on and started to try and dance. As he was staggering around he called to me, 'Come over here, I want you to dance with me.'

 Mum said, ' Its late, Alan, she needs to go back to bed .'

'Shut the fuck up, sue, if I want to dance with her I will.'

 Mum went into the kitchen leaving me with him. He grabbed me stinking of beer, his big hands holding my arms with a vice-like grip.

 When I was dancing with him he told me, 'If you keep me happy then you could help mum and I won't hurt her.'

He carried on dancing, mum came back in and was pulling me away.

'She's going to bed, Alan.' He went mad.

 He disappeared into the kitchen and when he came back he had a massive kitchen knife in his hand, and was charging towards mum with it.

 I don't know where my courage came from - I jumped in front of mum to stop him.

Looking at me he said, 'Maybe we should kill you, that would be one less mouth to feed, 'Nah I have got a better idea: lets just get rid of Katie - she eats too much and she'sfucking mouthy.'

He chucked the knife at mum; it just missed her hitting the wall behind her. He staggered back into the kitchen again.

"Why"

This time he returned into the lounge with a beer bottle in each hand. Mum shouted, ' Your pissed and you're not drinking in the house.'

He replied, 'You can fuck off sue. If I want a beer I will have a beer. Marie, you can sit here next to me.'

'She should be in bed, Alan, 'Mum yelled.

I did just as he instructed me to do. I was too scared not too.

He looked at mum, putting his arm round me and swigging on his beer. 'I like you, Marie, but you really piss me off when your naughty.'

I sat as still as I could and didn't answer him. He drunk the bottles dry and threw them on the floor,without another word got up and went to bed.

After that night I hated that letter coming. I knew exactly when it was due. Alan was always at the bedroom window looking for the postman.

There was always a shouting match when it came, always with the same outcome. He would storm out and come home in the early hours of the morning drunk, smashing windows so he could get into the house then smashing it up.

On another occasion, the letter had come and he was drunk. He had come home a lot earlier than normal, He kicked the front door in and came in to the lounge, where we was all watching TV.

'I am home early because I've run out of money and that's your fault, Sue.'

"Why"

He empted the shelves of all mum's Cliff Richard
records, throwing them all over the lounge floor,
stamping all over them laughing, smashing every one of
them to pieces.
He said, 'If I cant have my beer, you can't have your
beloved records.'
Mum always got a beating and always had new cuts and
bruises in the morning.
Alan wasn't giving mum any food money. Food had
become in short supply; me and Katie had to eat
whatever we was given. During the week we had hot
dinners at school, mum told us try and get second
helpings at lunch time. At the weekend we had a dinner
at home; like normal kids I hated vegetables.
Alan would sit and watch us, and making us eat
everything that was on our plate. If we left anything, the
same food would be on our plate for tea the next day,
then the next until it was eaten.
One weekend we was all called to the table for dinner. I
was first in the dinning room. Alan came in with my
plate, as usual dropping my sausages on the floor. He
picked them up and put them back and laughed. I sat at
the table looking at my plate with everyone else eating .
Mum saying, 'Come on Marie, eat up.'
I said, 'I am not hungry.'
Alan pipped up,' Come on, girl, we can't afford to waste
food.'
So I picked up my fork and started to pick at the mash
and peas, trying to avoid eating the sausages.

"Why"

I could feel Alan's eyes fixed on me he grunted, 'Eat the
sausages.'
I had a bite out of both of them then said, ' I am full up.'
My plate was taken away from me and I was sent to my
room. The same plate of sausages, mash and peas, was
put in front of me every night for a week. By the end of
the week the food was going mouldy, but he still put it in
front of me. Alan picked up a forkful of mouldy food
from my plate and forced it into my mouth. The smell
of the mouldy food on the fork made me vomit. He
slammed the fork down on to the plate. Lashing out he
punched me in the head, knocking me on to the chair
next to me.
'Stay there, Marie.' he ordered.
 He picked up my plate of food and put it in the bin
then he started dishing me out a good beating, while
calling me a waste full little bastard. More punches and
slaps came raining on to my body; I fell from the chair.
Like a sitting duck. I was trapped on the floor in the
corner of the dining room. He was standing over me and
then the kicking started, winding me and battering my
body. There wasn't one part of my body that he missed
that night. He kicked me so hard, I hit my head on the
wall and was knocking me unconscious.
I don't know how long I was there. But when I came
round I was on my own on the dining floor. My body
racked with pain: I touched my head and feeling a big
lump under my hair. I walked through the lounge, where
mum and Alan was sitting watching TV - they both just
stared at me as I passed him.

"Why"

I started to hate and dread mealtimes. I was thankful when I arrived and there was only a sandwich.

A few weeks had pasted after that incident. I arrived home from school but Katie hadn't yet arrived home. I went into the kitchen and made myself a sandwich as usual. While sitting up at the dining table I looked up at the clock hanging on the wall over the cooker.

It was almost half past four and still no sign of Katie. I was getting worried now so I asked mum, 'Where is Katie?'

That was when mum dropped the bomb shell, telling me: 'Katie has gone to live with your dad and Mary, Alan has made his mind up and it was Katie that had to be sent to Dad's.'

'Why Katie and not me?'

'Alan has made his mind up, it had to Katie because she was the biggest and she ate more than you, Marie.'

I replied that ' I would eat less if it meant Katie didn't have to leave home.'

Me and Katie weren't close but I was going to miss her loads; after all she was my big sister.

Mum just turned and walked away without saying anything else.

I went upstairs and walked into Katie's bedroom. All her stuff had gone, her bed had no covers on and her wardrobe was empty.

So that was that, there was three of us now. I wondered if life would get better. Maybe the rows over money would stop, As there was less of strain on the money and one less mouth to feed, but yet again I was wrong .

44

"Why"

It was the first bath night since Katie had gone. I was in my bedroom waiting for my turn.

Then mum shouted out, 'Marie get in the bath quickly because the water was getting cold.'

I passed Mum, wrapped in a towel on the landing, as I rushed into the bathroom. I undressed myself and lowered myself into the almost cold cloudy water.

I was trying to wash as quietly and as quickly as possible, so I could hear if there was any footsteps on the stairs, while watching the bathroom door handle for the slightest movement. I was nervous at every sound in my life now, because I never knew when the next beating was coming.

But if I knew what was going to happen next I'd've taken a beating any day.

I was lying down in the bath, with my ears under the water to wash my hair. When I spotted the door handle move down, the door opened and Alan walked in.

I jumped out of the bath as soon as I could - I didn't want to go under the water again. I didn't want to be naked in front of him either.

I grabbed the nearest towel and wrapped it tightly around me. He was standing right next to me, so I bolted for the door but it was locked.

He then continued to tell me, 'I have another present for you.'

He instructed me: 'Take the towel off.'

'No.' He yanked at the towel.

I tried to keep hold of it but I wasn't strong enough.

'Do as I say, Marie and nobody will get hurt.'

"Why"

' Now get on your knees in front of me.'

Then he unzipped his trousers and got his man thing out.

'Put this in your mouth and stuck it like a lolly,' he said.

I shut my eyes wishing I was somewhere else. I put it in my mouth; I only had a small mouth. It was only just going in, then he pushed really hard forcing it right in my mouth. I gagged as it hit the back of my throat. He grabbed the hair on the back of my head. Controlling my movements by pulling on my hair, he started to make my head move backwards and forwards. I couldn't stop gagging, my eyes watering and tears rolling down my cheeks from the pain of him pulling my hair. Then I felt something in the back of my throat and he pulled himself out straight away.

I was sick all over the floor; the taste was horrible.

'Clean yourself up. If you don't want mum to get a beating then I would keep this our secret.'

He then unlocked the door and left. I just fell into a soaking wet ball on the stone cold floor, I couldn't move.

After a while I got to my knees and started to clean my vomit up. I was asking myself why did he do these things to me that I didn't like?

Why did he hate me? Why didn't mum take me away from it all?

Then I heard someone coming up the stairs.

It was mum. she asked, 'Are you all right?' as she walked in.

Telling me, 'Alan said you wasn't well and had been sick.'

46

"Why"

I looked at her saying nothing. Mum said 'Its probably
best you go straight to bed and get yourself better for
tomorrow as you have school.'
 I walked passed mum still saying nothing and went into
my bedroom and got into bed. I lay there in bed, I
couldn't get rid of the horrible taste in my mouth. I was
still gagging and trying my best not to be sick.
Eventually I managed to fall asleep.
I couldn't wait to get to school in the morning. When I
arrived sally came running up to me all excited.
 'We are going on a camping holiday and my mum was
going to asks your mum if you can come with us.'
I hoped with all my heart that I would be allowed to go
camping with sally's family. I'd never been on a
holiday , not that it was Mum's fault - we just couldn't
afford one. I always wondered what a holiday would be
like.
 The six weeks holidays were coming up so I was
unhappy that I wouldn't be seeing sally for a long time.
However if I was allowed to go on the camping holiday
it would break this up. I think I knew what the answer
was going to be, but I was wrong - it was worse.
 At the end of the day when the bell rang, me and sally
ran out of school fast as we could together - there
waiting was sally's mum.
 We all walked out of the gate and up the road towards
home; as we pasted the sweet shop Sally's mum give us
thirty pence each telling us, 'no bubble gum.'

"Why"

We went in and got a big bag of penny sweets each, then carried on walking to my house, so she could ask my mum about me going away with them. We knocked on the door when we arrived at my house and mum answered the door. The two mums stood on the door step talking. Sally's mum asked 'would it be ok for Marie to come camping with us in the school holidays?'
My world feel apart after I heard the words mum said next.
Mum replied, 'I am really sorry but we are moving away in the school holidays, so I am sorry but I will have to say no, but hopefully the two girls could still keep in touch.'
I said, 'bye' to sally and her mum and then they walked away, I hated mum that night and I couldn't get my head round that we was moving.
On the last day before the school broke up for the holidays was great - we didn't have to do any work, we just played games all day. The only thing missing that day was sally - she had already gone on her holidays. Even after one day I was missing sally already.
The bell rang for the end of the day and I walked home on my own.
I turned into our road, I could see a big white van parked outside our house.
When I walked into the house I noticed mum had been busy.
There was boxes everywhere with all our belongings in, the birds from the garden were in cages and the fish splashing around in buckets.

"Why"

I asked mum, 'Will I still be going to the same school with sally?'

Mum said, 'No we are moving to another town, so we would have a new house and you will have a new school and new friends.'

Mum and Alan and another man was loading all our stuff in the back of the van.

Mum asked me, 'It will be time to go soon, are you excited?'

I wanted to shout out no and run, I didn't; I just stood there watching box after box being stacked into the back of the van. While they finished putting the last bits on the van, I went into the nearly empty house and up to my bedroom.

My room was empty apart from a black bin bag in the corner.

Then I spotted my doll's arm hanging out of the top. I shouted down to mum. when she answered I said, 'You have forgotten a bag in my room.'

only to be told, 'No that's all rubbish, Marie.'

I looked back at the bag and ran over to it, taking my doll out. I couldn't let her be rubbish even if her head was broken off. So I put her in my school bag before mum found out.

I was standing looking out of my bedroom window; Alan and the other man was sitting on the kerb having a fag and a cup of tea.

The van's doors was still wide open; the van was full up with our belongings. Mum called out, ' Everything is on the van now - its time to lock up and go.'

"Why"

Chapter Five

Mum locked the front door. The man driving the van was already sitting in the driver's seat with the engine running. As I walked down the path Alan told me, 'You will have to sit in the back with the furniture, Marie.' I went to the back of the van and hopped up.
Alan said, 'Right, Marie, sit on the arm of the sofa and hold the buckets of fish between your legs.' Said Alan He closed one door. Just before he closed the other door he looked at me with his eyes bulging.
'If you let the buckets fall over you will be for it.' He slammed the second door shut.
It was pitch black in the back of the van once the doors were shut. I heard Alan and mum get in with the driver, then he pulled away.
Just as he did the van lurched forward; all our belongings started rattling and shaking.

"Why"

The noise was deafening, the water splashed out of the
buckets, the birds flapping like mad in their cage.
As the van picked up speed It was getting harder to stay
sitting, especially when we went round a corner. The
water was splashing more and more; every time we went
over a bump in the road..
My trousers and feet were getting wetter and wetter; the
noise from the birds was deafening.
They must have been panicking, but not as much as I
was trying to keep the buckets from falling over. I could
still hear the voices, from the front where mum, Alan
and the other man was.
Our stuff was moving around more the longer the
journey went on - nothing had been tied down.
We must have stopped at some traffic lights - when we
pulled away everything lurched again. The bird cage
came crashing down on my legs. I tried to push it back
upright. As I did a box came from nowhere hitting me
on shoulder. I was stuck like that for a while until the
van leaned to one side and I managed to push the bird
cage back up.
My shoulder aching and hurting, I pushed the box off
me. It was really heavy I had to push with all my might
to move it.
The box feel down beside me and I heard something
smash, the sound of the breaking glass filled me with
fear as it was bound to be my fault. We seemed to be
driving ages, then suddenly everything seemed to stop
moving. I couldn't hear the engine any more, as the
doors opened up.

"Why"

Shielding my eyes from the bright sunlight, I looked down at the fish. Thankfully they were still all in their buckets but most of water had been spilt .

I climbed out of the van, the sunshine blinding me at first, until my eyes adjusted.

Then I saw the house that I would end up hating; it would end up being like a prison cell to me.

When mum unlocked the front door, we went inside to have a look around. It was bigger than the house we had just left. Downstairs there was a small hallway as I entered the house, with a door that lead into the lounge. I pushed open the door and was standing in the massive empty lounge. The stairs were in the lounge, with a storage cupboard under them. I opened the cupboard door to be noisy, I poked my head in to the cupboard - it was tiny inside I couldn't even stand up straight without banging my head. As there was nothing exciting in there I started to explore the rest of the house. I found my way through the dining room into the small kitchen. Looking out of the back door window, at the tall grass in the garden, I tried the door handle but it was locked. I went and explored the upstairs and looked around the bedrooms. There was three bedrooms: two big ones and a small one just big enough for a bed.

Just then Alan was coming up the stairs with a box in his hands. I thought I'd try my luck so asked, 'Can I have one of the big rooms?'

He laughed and said, 'I don't think so.'

Then he nodded at the rooms one by one. 'That big one is mine and mum's room, that big one is for my weights, that little one is yours.'

"Why"

I didn't dare argue, so I went in to my new room to have a better look. There was a door inside my room; I opened it. There a this big metal tank and loads of pipes inside. I lifted the lid on the tank; it was full to the brim with water.

As I stood looking into the garden from the bedroom window, already I was starting to hate this house. I heard mum shout, 'Stop playing about up there, you can come down and help.'

Mum gave me a box when I reach the van outside. She said, 'Be careful with that one, Marie- it sounds like something inside has smashed already.'

Alan and the other man started to unload the furniture. We carried on backwards and forwards until everything was out the van and in the house.

The man diving the van said, 'Thanks, bye.' to Alan. I wanted to run after him and tell him to take me back, but he disappeared.

The rest of the day and into the night, we all moved stuff around until everything had a place. The sofa went on the wall of the stairs over the cupboard door. The armchairs went on the other wall with the empty fish tank; the TV went on a cabinet in the corner of the room.

Although most things were unpacked, when I went up to bed there was still boxes stacked up in the dining room. The fish had been emptied from their buckets into the bath, where they would be for weeks to come.

"Why"

I lay in bed, the light from the moon in the clear
summer night sky filling my room. My new room
looking more like a bedroom, now some of my stuff was
in it, but I still missed my old one back in Basildon. I lay
there for what seemed like ages listening the strange
whooshing and popping noises that were coming from
the cupboard. I couldn't get use to them, it Just didn't
feel right, but I finally fell asleep.

We had been in the house for a few weeks. Alan had
gone out before I had got up. He was still out come tea
time; Mum called me to the table.

She said, 'I bet he has been in the pub all day,or with
some tart.'

I said, 'Didn't he say where he was going, mum?'

She said, 'No, he just got up and went out.'

She carried on moaning about him being out all day,
getting more and more angry. I was thinking, I am glad
he has been out all day - I was wishing he had gone for
good.

As he was out I asked, 'Can I watch some TV after I've
done my chores?'

Mum said, 'You can sit with me for a little while, Marie,
then its bed time.'

I was sitting on the floor in the lounge watching TV,
with mum keeping an eye on the clock, huffing and
puffing that Alan still Wasn't home.

Mum said, 'Its starting to get dark outside, Marie you
can go to bed soon.'As she finished talking the the front
door opened.

Mum flew out of the chair when Alan walked into the
house. He came into the lounge carrying a big TV in his
arms.

"Why"

'Where the fucking hell have you been all day?
Where did you get that from ? we have no money,' mum
screamed.
 He said, 'I found it in a skip - let's plug it in to see if it
works.'
Mum went into one. 'Don't give me all that bollocks; you
have been with a woman or in the pub or maybe fucking
both.'
Alan said, 'I'm not telling you again. I've been out
looking in skips, Sue.'
Mum started looking all round his neck and smelling
him.
'Just because you haven't got a love bite doesn't mean
you haven't been fucking around. And another thing
Alan we have been in this house for a couple of weeks
now and none of us have had a bath, because the fish are
still in it.'
Alan just ignored her, plugging in the TV.
He flicked the switch and the TV screen came on. Alan
was over the moon with himself.
Mum sent me to bed, For most of the night I heard them
shouting at each other. Mum accusing him of seeing
someone else, his voice getting louder. All of a sudden it
all stopped.
The next morning I was eating my Breakfast,When mum
came into the Kitchen Yet again sporting another Black
eye.
I asked, 'Where is Alan, Mum?'
She said, 'He has gone out, probably to see that tart
again.' I was just happy he was out again.

"Why"

He came home just before tea time. As soon as he was indoors mum let rip at him again.

'Didn't you have enough of your slag yesterday?'

'I've been looking around for fucking skips again, you stupid bitch,'he replied

Mum yelled, 'I don't believe you Alan- you have come home with nothing.'

Alan raised his voice. 'For fuck sake, I've been around the industrial estate near the docks looking but I will have to go back there at night.'

'I am telling you Alan, I want to know who this woman is now fucking tell me.'

'I've not been with a woman, Sue,' said Alan

Mum said, 'Well your not going out looking in skips tomorrow.'

'yes I fucking am, sue.'

Mum said, 'Well you can take Marie with you.'

Alan said, 'What? to report back to you, sue?'

Mum said, 'yes.'

The next morning Alan was waiting for me in the kitchen.

'Eat your breakfast, Marie,we are going out'

Mum came in, 'Right, Marie, I want you to tell me where he goes and who he speaks to, especially if he talks to ladies.'

Alan was hurrying me up to get out of the door.

As soon as we was out of sight of the house, he grabbed me, putting his nose on mine.

'You tell mum, what I tell you to say about what goes on while we are out looking in skips.'

Full of fear I said 'ok.'

"Why"

Then he said, 'If you tell her different, the next day we go out I will kill you and throw you in the river, then go back and kill your mum, do you hear me, Marie?'
'yes.' I whispered
'That's a good little girl.'he said
I asked, 'What are skips Alan?'
He said, 'They are big metal bins that people put stuff in they don't want any more, You can help me look - I will lift you up into the skip then jump in behind you.'
We had been out most of the day, only finding a couple of skips that had rubble and dirt in them.
On our way home we found a skip with all sorts of rubbish in it.
Alan jumped in. 'This could come in handy, Marie.'
He lifted up an old rusty push bike and threw it to the ground.
Sitting on it he said, ' It needs a bit of work but I think I can sort it out – but we will have to push it home.'
As we was walking home he said, 'Right Marie you can tell mum the truth today.'
We got home. He took the bike out into the garden and started to try and fix it. While mum was cooking dinner she closed the back door. 'Where did you go today?'
I said, 'Just walked around the streets looking in skips, mum. he found the bike in the last skip we looked in.'
Mum replied, 'ok Marie.'

"Why"

Alan came in. 'All it needed was some air in the tyres and a drop of oil, now its as good as new.'
Mum said, 'I Bet you only went round looking for skips because Marie was with you, Alan.'
' I go looking in skips for things that I can sell to get some money Sue.'
We was out nearly everyday for the rest of the school holidays.
I had to sit on the back of the bike, just riding around the streets and going behind the shops in the high street. At the weekends we would go to the industrial estate, as there wasn't anybody about.
Sometimes we were going out when the postman was coming along and heading back when it was getting dark .
I hated the skips because they were smelly and dirty; the big ones on the industrial estate were running a live with rats. Now and again we did get some good stuff out of them. Most of the stuff he found he would go and try to sell straight away.
I had to wait outside the pubs for ages while he went in. He would come out stinking of beer saying, ' Best not tell mum what we have done today.' Then we would go and look for another skip.
Before we got home he would stop. 'Tell mum we didn't find anything today and don't tell her we have been to the pubs.' One morning we was out, the first skip we came to Alan found some records and a small record player.

"Why"

Alan said, 'Lets go round a few pubs and try to sell this. if nobody wants it and you're good you can have this in your room.'

We must have gone to at least five pubs in Tilbury but he always came back out with them.

On the way home he said ' ok as you have been good you can have it in your bedroom.'

I was happy: I had a record player but I didn't like the idea it had come from him out of a smelly, dirty skip.

When we got home, Mum told Alan, ' She can't go out tomorrow - she's got school. Because she can't go I want you to start on that pond so we can use the bath.'

Alan said, 'No I am going out but I will start the pond soon.'

Mum hit the roof. 'Now she's back at school you're off round to that slag's again then, Alan.'

Yet again I lay in bed listening to them shouting at each other. The following morning was the day I had been dreading.

Its was time for me to go to my new school. On the first day mum said, 'I will walk you to school today as its your first day.'

After breakfast mum brushed my hair and plaited it for me.

Although I liked my hair up mum didn't do it gently. I kept moving because mum was hurting my head, then I felt this pain. Mum lashed out hitting me with the brush saying, 'keep fucking still.'

Then I felt the brush strike my head again and mum shouting, 'You've made me break my brush now.'

She finished doing my hair with the brush that didn't have a handle any more.

"Why"

We left for school. I thought maybe because it was a new school mum would take me every morning, but that didn't happen. It was a longer walk to school than it used to be. When we got to school the playground was empty. Mum stopped at the gate.

Mum told me, 'We must be late, you have to walk across the playground and into the office, tell them your name and that you are new at Henry Green, tell them mum couldn't stop as she would be late for work.'

I don't know where Mum went but she didn't work. The lady in the office took me by the hand to a classroom; she opened the classroom door and took me in, telling my new teacher: 'This is Marie beech.'

The teacher took my hand and made me stand in front of everyone for the class to say hello. The teacher told me to sit at a table in the middle of the classroom with seven other children. Right from the start I hated this school and every thing about it.

No one spoke to me at play time, I just sat on the little wall.

I watched everyone else play, thinking of my friend Sally.

I thought of her back at the table with the empty seat, where I wished and should have been. I keep myself to myself and wished I was invisible.

One day I had got home from school, I was told by mum, 'You have to stay with Alan this evening and you better be good, because I am going out to bingo, I will be going more than Monday nights; it will be three times a week from now on.'

"Why"

Every time she went bingo I was left with Alan. Most of the time he left me alone in my bedroom playing records.

Just after mum left One night, he told me to come downstairs saying, 'I am going to play a game with you. You have to lie on the floor and try and stay as still as you can and keep your eyes closed.'

I did as he told me: I lay on the floor and closed my eyes tight. Getting really nervous and my heart beating faster, I couldn't see him, but all of a sudden there was a hand over my mouth and a heavy weight on top of me. I kept still - I couldn't move. I felt his hand pulling up my school dress and tugging at my knickers yanking them down. Once he had ripped my knickers off me he forced my legs apart. I felt a pain so bad I thought I was going to die. The heavy weight started to move on top of me. He was pushing inside me but it was more painful than last time. I felt the pain in my belly and he was doing that heavy breathing as well, the movement got faster and faster, then it stopped and the weight lifted off me, My mouth was uncovered.

Alan told me, ' Fuck off back upstairs.'

When I was walking back up the stairs I felt wet down below, so I went to the toilet.

Locking the door even though I knew I would be in trouble for locking the door if I got caught. I didn't care. I sat on the toilet and had a wee; the burning pain inside me made me cry. When I finished I wiped myself and there was blood on the tissue, I actually thought I was dying.

"Why"

The next day I could hardly walk; each step I took I got a pain shooting up inside me. Every time I went for a wee the stinging was just too much, so I had to hold myself . Finally my bladder couldn't take any more, I wet myself .

 Mum went mad. 'You are seven and a half and you should know better at your age...'as she slapped me.
The rows didn't stop; Alan was still taking all the money and leaving no money for food. If he had no money he was disappearing all day telling mum he was looking for skips.

I thought why did Katie have to go, if nothing was going to change.

Eventually mum got the giro made out in her name so he couldn't cash it in. This made things worst for her and me.

The first time the money came and Alan didn't get any of it, he smashed up the front room. The sofa was up on its end and the plants were pulled out of their pots and chucked across the room, then he went for mum.

I was just coming down to do my chores when I walked into the front room. There was Alan holding mum and saying, 'I am going to put your head through the fish tank if you don't give me the money.'

But for some reason she didn't give him any money. He punched her in the face, then went to smash her head into the tank.

But me being stupid as normal shouted 'please stop,' tears running down my face. Then he stopped and just kicked the tank instead, smashing the glass, the water and the fish pouring on to the floor.

"Why"

After that Alan picked up the TV. I thought it was going to be the next thing across the room. But he didn't chuck it he just carried it out of the house and went. This became what happened when the money came and he didn't get any. He would smash up the house and take something to sell. the trouble with this was he had to keep replacing them after he had come off the drink. So in the evenings after school off me and him would go and find more stuff.

"Why"

Chapter Six

I had been at my new school for a few weeks and still
hadn't made any friends. I had become a very quite and
frightened little girl. I think this stopped me trying to
make friends. I missed my friend sally so much; I would
often just sit on the wall out in the playground thinking
of her and the fun we use to have.
It didn't help that I started to smell.
Alan was still building a pond for the fish that were still
in the bath; it was nearly four weeks before it was
finished. I got the nickname 'smelly' before to long, I
hated school and my home life. At least when I lived
near sally, I had some happy times during the day but
nothing made me smile any more.
At the weekends, I was still made to go with Alan when
he went out looking for stuff. On one of these trips we
headed for the high street; we pasted the service road
that lead to the back of the shops. Reaching the high
street we crossed the road. Right in front of us was a
sweet shop. 'Marie, wait outside while I go in.' Alan told
me.
He came out with a bag of penny sweets and handed
them to me.
He said, 'We are not going to the skips today; instead we
are going to see some of my friends.'
We carried on walking for a while, going down lots of
different roads that I hadn't seen before.

"Why"

We turned into a street; one of the first houses we came to was a grotty, run down dump.

Alan said, 'Here we are Marie.'

The gate hanging off and the garden full of beer cans.

The ripped brown nets curtains hanging at flaky painted window frames.

Every window on the front of the house, had a broken pane of glass that had been covered with a board. We made our way up the path, pushing through the over grown hedge to get to the door. Alan knocked on the rotten door, The curtain was slightly pulled back in the downstairs window. Then I could hear lots of door bolts being released.

Then someone was tugging at the door, a man's head appeared in the opening.

Alan said, 'Will she do then? '

The man looked at me and smiled, showing his yellow and brown teeth.

He opened the door wider and Alan pushed me into the house. As soon as we was in the man slammed the door shut locking the bolts behind us.

We followed the man into the front room. There were six other men, sitting on chairs and some sitting on the floor, all drinking tins of beer. I felt all of their eyes glaring at me looking me up and down as I entered the room.

All of them had matted hair, with filthy black hands and clothes that had all sorts of stains on them. The floor had loads of empty crushed tins all over it. There was rubbish and what looked like dogs hairs everywhere I looked .

"Why"

The air was thick with smoke with ashtrays spilling over with ash and dog ends. The sofas and carpet were all shiny with grime and dirt. They was all watching something with naked people, on the TV in the corner. One of the men moved along the sofa and patted the seat beside him 'Come and sit next to me, little one.'
Alan said, 'No she can stand over there in the corner sofas; are only for adults in our house.'
Even if I was allowed to sit on the sofa, I think I would of choose to stand because of the state of the place. I definitely wasn't going to sit on the floor so I stood in the corner of the room. Trying not to been seen, I didn't want to do anything that would make Alan mad. The same man handed Alan a can of beer, he started drinking one can after the other,while talking to the other men
After standing there for a while, the man that had let us into the house entered the room. He walked over to Alan; I heard him say ' Ok the room is ready, you can take her up.'
 Alan stood up and placed he's drink on the table and walked over to me. Gripping my hand tight, Nearly pulling me off my feet, he dragged me towards the door. I was hoping and thought we where leaving, but he dragged me upstairs.
As we reached the top, my fingers hurting from his crushing grip.
He pulled me into a bedroom; it was pitch black. There was a blanket up at the window. I could only just see the brown marks and stains on the mattress on the bed frame.

"Why"

The only light getting into the room, was from the dim light bulb on the landing.

Alan said, 'Be a good girl, sit on the edge of the bed and don't move. '

He then left and closed the door. I was looking at the little light that was coming under the door.

I jumped at the click of the light switch; The light from under the door disappeared throwing the room into total darkness. My eyes wide open straining to see in the darkness. Sitting on a bed that felt damp and smelt like someone had wet it,I was so frightened.

Listening to muffled voices from downstairs, thinking I don't want to be here, I didn't know what was going happen next. I panicked as I heard the stairs creaking under someone's foot steps. Then the door knob rattling as if someone was having trouble opening it. There was a thud and the door opened. I could just make out the silhouette of a figure, in the faint light that was coming from downstairs.

'Alan?' I asked

'Shut up.' said a strange voice.

The figure Stepped into the room, Closing the door behind them.

I sat on the edge of the bed in the darkness trying to listen where they were in the room. Moving my head around trying to see in the dark, I couldn't see them. All of a sudden, I felt something cold tighten round my neck pulling me backwards. I ended up lying on my back, I think I stopped breathing because I was so scared.

My air being cut off, all the time this thing that felt like a belt getting tighter round my neck, I could feel hands touching my body.

"Why"

Suddenly my trousers where being undone and pulled at, then my knickers. My legs being forced apart and a hand between them.

The weight on top of me was getting heavier, then a hard push and then the excruciating pain between my legs and in my belly hit me.

I let myself cry without making a sound. I knew if I couldn't see this person face then they couldn't see mine.

After the heavy breathing and moving had stopped,the belt loosened. The weight was taken off me and the air was allowed back in .The door opened and the figure left closing the door behind them. Pulling myself up I sat on the bed. Getting down on my knees to feel around on the floor in the dark for my clothes.

The bedroom door opened; this time there was a larger figure in the door way.

They said, ' Get back on the bed, we aren't done with you yet.'

I was then subjected to the exact same treatment as before. Lying on the bed crying without a sound, the pain getting more and more unbearable with the punishment my body was taking. Trying to imagine, being somewhere else any where but here. Every time the punishment stopped the door opened and the figure left, only to be replaced by another figure at the bedroom door and it would all start again until they had all used me.

Lying on the bed racked with pain, trying to find reasons why they was doing this to me, I heard the click of a light switch in the hallway.

"Why"

The door swung open, I turned my head to face Alan
standing at the door way.

As he walked in ordering me ' Stand up.'

I had to gather all the strength I had left to lift myself up
off the stained mattress, Finally getting to my feet with
my legs wobbling.

Alan came closer. I thought he was going to push me
back on to the bed

He said, ' Come on hurry up.' My legs just wouldn't
work, as I stood there shaking.

He dragged me to the bathroom barking out another of
his orders, 'Clean yourself up we have got to get home.'

He closed the door behind him. Listening to him going
down the stairs I switched the light on and locked the
door.

 I looked around at the bathroom, at the tiles hanging off
the wall.

The window covered in mould and the toilet seat
missing. The bath and sink had thick dirty marks under
the taps right down to the plug hole.

Looking around for some toilet paper to clean myself up
with. I found some in the cabinet on the wall, closing the
cabinet door ,catching a glimpse of my red face and
puffy eyes in the mirror. Cleaning myself up the best as I
could with the tissue. I didn't wee because I didn't want
the stinging. I know It would of stung, - it felt the same
as when Alan did the same to me.

"Why"

We left soon after. When we were nearing the front door, the man we saw first at the front door said to Alan, 'Sweet little thing you have there. '

Alan replied, 'Yes she's mine.'

The walk home was painful; my legs wouldn't work they felt heavy and felt like jelly. With every step the soreness and burning down below got worst.

As the cars went passed us, I wanted one of them to run Alan over.

I didn't want him in my life any more.

Finally we reached home Alan said, 'you can fuck off to bed now.'

I wanted to wash; all I could smell was sweat on me. I felt dirty but it wasn't a bath night So I went straight to my room.

As I was getting ready for bed, it came to me. I ripped off all my clothes, throwing them in to a pile on the floor. Going to the cupboard that was in my room and opened door, I slid open the lid on the big tank.

Using my top as flannel, I dunked it in to make it wet and wipe myself clean. I washed myself all over trying to get rid of the smell of the men.

The water was freezing cold but I didn't care; I just wanted to be clean.

I was gathering my clothes up when I got to my knickers - they were full of blood.

I hadn't noticed it before; I had ripped my clothes off so quickly, just wanting to be clean and throw them away from me.

"Why"

I rolled them up and put them in the bottom of one of my drawers.

After I was all done I climbed into bed. I tried so hard to sleep. The uncontrollably crying keeping me awake; sleep never came easy that night.

Whenever I started to drift off, I would get flash backs of what had happened, being startled thinking someone was coming into my room at every sound I heard.

When I woke up in the morning, my throat was really sore. It was painfully every time I swallowed, my voice squeaking.

I walked down stairs and went to have my breakfast; There was only toast to have. It would have been to painful to eat it so I went without.

Mum was in bed still but Alan was in the garden. He came back in just as I was putting my shoes on; he walked over to me and grabbed my hair, to make me face him and said, 'You was a good girl yesterday but don't forget your mine. '

He let go and walked off to the bottom of the garden. I ran and grabbed my school bag and left the house in seconds.

I arrived at the school gates and walked past without stopping.

When I had passed the school I started to run; I wanted to run and keep running. I came to a small park that I had not seen before .

I sat on the swings and cried my eyes out. I was scared about the school telling my mum that I had not turned up.

"Why"

I just didn't care I spent all day there; the trouble was I didn't have a watch and was late home that night. Mum was at home waiting for me when I got in, straight away mum started shouting.

Alan dragged me to the dining table and force me over; holding me down he started hitting me with his belt. I didn't cry or make a sound.

I wouldn't cry any more in front of him. Just before he told me to go to my room he leaned over me and said into my ear, 'Your real punishment will be tonight.' Then I was kicked all the way to the stairs; he pushed me so hard I fell over. While I was on the floor he kicked me all over my body. My body ached all over, again my bottom was so sore. I got back to my feet, then he gave me one more boot in the leg; he had given me a dead leg and I fell to the floor again. Leaning down he said, 'You better get up them stairs now.' I crawled up the stairs with him watching me all the way up.

Gingerly lowering myself on to my bed, my bottom touched the bed; I jumped up straight away because of the pain from the beating. I got into bed; I just lay there thinking of Alan's warning running round my thoughts. I fell asleep. Before I knew it I was woken up by my covers being pulled off me. I opened my eyes; the room was pitch black. The bed covers stopped moving, I could feel hands touching me. I tried to curl up in to a ball. One of the hands reached to my mouth and pushed hard. I couldn't breathe. The other hand straightening my body out.

"Why"

The heavy weight on top of me again. The smell and then movement; he was using my tiny body for his pleasure again.

I knew it was Alan from funny smell. After that night this happened nearly every night. I tried to tuck the bed covers around me, thinking if it was tucked in tight he wouldn't be able to get at me.

I kept my head under the covers, just looking out to look at the door to make sure it was closed .

I was wetting the bed at night because I would hold myself all night long.

I didn't want to move once I was tucked in. He came in and had his evil sick fun but because my bladder was full. I wet myself. He got off me, grabbing my hair and rubbed my face into the urine soaked bed and whispering in my ear, 'You are disgusting.'

On another one of these night's he said something to me. I had an idea he said he liked me because I was cuddly and that's was it. I had a thought that maybe if I wasn't fat he would leave me alone. So I went about to stop eating, which was easier than I thought because at home there was never a lot of food in the house.

Most of the time, I had to make myself a sandwich when I got in.

I would put breadcrumbs on a plate and wipe the butter with a knife so it looked like I had eaten.

The weather had started to change; outside it was getting colder because winter was on its way again. Even Christmas didn't enter my thoughts - I just focused on not eating.

"Why"

I wanted to be thin, because my seven year old mind thought this would fix everything because of what Alan had said to Katie . That year we had lots of snow, I hadn't been eating for about four weeks by now.

So I had started to lose weight, but every time I looked in the mirror, all I saw was a chubby me standing there.
The weather was freezing and I really started to feel it.
I never had a big winter coat, so maybe it was because of the small coat that I had on all year round. Or was it because I had lost so much weight, I had no fat to keep me warm.

School had two weeks left before we broke up for Christmas. I was dreading it. Alan had already got stocks of drink in the cupboards. I knew when he drunk his drink it turned him nasty and he wanted more drink. On the last day at school we had a Christmas party. I wasn't looking forward to Christmas; I only had sad memories of the last Christmas.

I just sat in the corner of the hall and thought of my friend that I missed everyday. I slowly walked home that day, when I arrived home I was in for a surprise and for once it was a nice one.

I walked into the house. Mum and Alan were sitting watching the TV.

They said, 'Make a cup of tea for us then come back in here, we have something to tell you.' As I was making the tea my mind was going into overdrive.

What was mum going to tell me?
I took their teas into the lounge, Then that's when mum said, 'Marie your going to your dad's for Christmas.'

"Why"

I said, 'How long before I go mum?'
She said, 'Five days, Marie, now go and make your sandwich.'
I hid my massive smile but inside I was dancing around. I left them sitting in the lounge and went to make my sandwich. After making it I sat at the table, making it look like I was eating it. Instead I was breaking it off and putting it in my pocket, so I could take it upstairs and get rid of it. I was still trying my best to lose weight.

"Why"

Chapter Seven

Mum said, 'Marie, you need to get an early night, Dad's coming for you tomorrow.'
Thinking about Christmas with my dad I rushed upstairs and jumped into bed.
 As soon as I was in bed the rowing started downstairs, the shouting getting louder and louder. I was waiting for the smashing and crashing to start but it never did. They were rowing for most of the night. I put my pillow over my head to muffle the rowing; finally I dropped off to sleep.
I was woken up by a hand over my mouth and my covers being pulled off of me. I could just make out Alan's face in the darkened room, leaning towards me stinking of beer and anger filling his eyes.
' You didn't think I would let you go to your dad's without giving you a present, do you?' Giving out a quiet laugh.
When he had finished using my body for his sick pleasure he got up and walked towards the door.
Stopping half way, he came back. 'Don't forget, this is our secret; if you tell your dad I will kill you, then kill your mum and dad. Remember, adults don't believe children.'
I lay there not moving. Why was he doing this to me every night?
Wishing he would kill me, then I wouldn't have to see him again.
 I didn't sleep for the rest of the night, lying on my bed waiting for it to get lighter outside.

"Why"

Once I heard that mum was up I got off my bed and went into the bathroom and had a wee.

The burning and stinging was getting worst every time Alan paid me a visit during the night. I hated that he did these things to me. After making myself clean the best I could, I went back into my room. At last Christmas eve had finally come and I was going to my Dad's.

It was still dark outside, I lay on my bed smiling, thinking about my dad coming for me and getting out of this house and away from Alan for a while.

I must have been daydreaming as my bedroom door opened.

Taking in a deep breath, the relief must have been all over my face when I saw that it was mum holding some clothes.

She said, 'I want you to wear these to your dad's, Marie.' I just sat looking at her thinking, how glad am I it was you opening my door.'Come on, Marie, get up and get dressed.'

I got up slowly trying not to moan and groan with the pain Alan had left my body in.

After I was dressed, I wasn't aloud downstairs early so I had to wait. Wiping the dampness off my window so I could see out into the frost covered garden, I sat at the window watching it get lighter outside. Excited but scared all at the same time.

Mum said, 'Go and make a cup of tea for me. Alan is still asleep so don't do him one ,while you're in the kitchen have breakfast.'

"Why"

'what time is dad getting me?' I asked, hoping it was soon.

She said,'I don't know, Marie.'

I left my room and walked downstairs. I went into the lounge and looked at the decorations still hanging up.

I carried on into the kitchen, switching on the kettle on and making myself some toast.

I tried not to have cereal these days, as It was harder to hide and take to my room. At lease I could put toast in my pockets.

On the mornings when there wasn't any bread, I would just put a bowl in the sink.

Putting a drop of milk in it, so it made It look like I had eaten something. I had to make toast because of the smell of it.

I left mum's tea on the kitchen side, heading back upstairs.

Passing mum on the way she said, 'Be quite in your room, try not to wake Alan.'

When I reached my room and shut the door behind me. I took the toast out my pocket and opened the cupboard. Reaching to the back, pulling out the carrier bag that had all my old food in.

I tucked the carrier bag into my over night bag, That had my clothes in for when I stayed at Dad's. I sat on my bed doing some drawings, wanting to stay out the way, as I could hear Alan was up now.

I liked it in my room - it was quite and I was left alone some of the time. I had been up for ages; the frost in the garden had melted away.

"Why"

Then I heard the sound that I had been waiting for: a knock at the front door and mum shout up to me, 'Come down, Marie, your dad's here; bring your bag down.'

I grabbed my bag and ran down the stairs. There standing in the lounge was dad and Mary with two girls.

Dad knelt down in front of me and said, 'Marie I would like you to meet Kerry and Rosie - these are Mary's daughters.'

I looked at them and they smiled back at me.

One of them had long brown hair like mine and the other girl had curly light hair.

Then I saw Katie standing behind Mary I went over and said, 'hi Katie, I've missed you.'

She said, 'Hi Marie, hows you?'

Dad said, 'Time to go, have you got everything you need, Marie? Get your shoes and coat,You might need your big coat -its cold outside '

Mum said, 'She hasn't got one at the moment - she ripped it at school.' I looked at mum and we both knew it was a lie.

We left the house and walked to the car that was parked outside. dad said, 'Marie and Rosie, you two will have to sit in the boot.'

We all climbed in to the car. As we pulled away I looked back at my house. I was worrying about mum, being alone with Alan and all his drink, but happy I was getting away from Alan.

As we all sat in the car, me and Rosie were chatting. She was moaning, 'It's always me that has to sit in the boot when there is a lot of us.'

"Why"

Kerry and Katie joined in with our chat, leaning over the back seat in to the boot, all of them firing questions at me. I found out that Kerry was two years older than me and Rosie was a year younger than me.

We seemed to be on a motorway for ages; there was cars everywhere. As we got nearer to Basildon the traffic stopped and we just crawled along.

Katie kept asking, 'How long before we get home? I need a wee.'

Dad said, 'The roads are busy with everyone trying to get home for Christmas but we shouldn't be long.'

The drive was much longer than my first trip in Dad's car. My bum was getting numb by the time we stopped and arrived at Dad's house. Dad opened the back door so me and Rosie could get out. we all walked towards the house, Katie running, saying, 'Hurry up and let me in. I followed everyone in. Dad said, 'Kerry, show Marie where she will be sleeping and where to put her bag.'

Kerry said, 'Come up with me, Marie. This is Rosie's room you can share with her; me and Katie are in that room.'

I stood in Rosie's room with my mouth open.

There was posters on the wall, toys everywhere and lovely warm carpet on the floor. I couldn't wait to spend a night in a nice warm cosy room. Kerry went back downstairs. I stayed in the bedroom sitting on the bed. Looking around the bedroom thinking Rosie doesn't know how lucky she is.

I heard dad shout up, 'Marie the girls are watching a film - do you fancy it as well?'

"Why"

I walked downstairs and into the lounge, everyone
sitting watching A film with father Christmas in. I sat on
the floor. Dad said, 'Come up here on the sofa. '
I must of looked shocked Dad didn't say anything.
 Mary said, 'There's a tin of chocolates on the table-
everyone help yourselves.' I watched the other three girls
get up and pick some sweets out of the tin. But I didn't
help myself to the chocolates.
Dad kept giving me some chocolates saying, 'Help
yourself, Marie, they are for everyone get in there before
the are all gone.' I had a couple of chocolates but gave
the others to Rosie. Everyone could do what they
wanted. I think I was waiting for Dad to start hitting or
beating someone for something. The lounge was
Beautiful, with all the Christmas decorations and in one
corner there was a big Christmas tree.
 While I sat there I could smell something cooking. Not
once was I asked to make a tea or ordered to do
something. When the film finished Mary called, 'Dinner
is ready, get up the table.'
Then I panicked because we all sat up at the table, even
the adults. How was I going to hide my food? It smelt
and looked lovely but I couldn't get fat, I couldn't start
eating.
 We had crackers to pull and inside were hats that
everyone wore. There were napkins on the table. I put
mine on my lap and had an idea to slip the food into it,
wrapping it up when no one was looking.
 Rosie didn't eat her vegetables. I just watched and was
wondering why she wasn't forced to eat them up.

81

"Why"

After dinner I carried my plate into the kitchen. I started to run the water to wash up, I was told by Dad and Mary, 'Go and play Marie we can do this.'

I walked upstairs and went to take the wrapped up napkin out of my pocket. Just as I was going to, Rosie, Kerry and Katie said, 'Come and play.' They ran back downstairs.
I opened my overnight bag and stuffed the food in to the carrier bag. Then I went downstairs to find the girls - they were in the front room. They was playing music and singing into this stick that was attached with a wire to a box that was playing a tape.
We all had lots of fun and sang loads of songs, then when we got bored of that we did each others hair. After a while dad came in and said, 'Who is having the first shower? you're the guest, Marie you can have the first one.'
Dad came up with me and said, 'You have to run the taps together until the water is ok.'
Then he left and told me to 'Shout down when your finished so someone else can have their turn '.
The water was clean and warm; I enjoyed it so much I was in there ages. Someone was knocking on the door, which made me jump. I thought I was in trouble. I jumped out and wrapped a towel round me. I opened the door - it was Mary she said, 'We was worried about you.'
I said, 'Sorry, Mary, I will get my nightie on.'
She said, 'Its no problem, Marie, we just wondered if you was ok.'
I walked into Rosie's room and got ready for bed.

"Why"

When I had my nightie on I climbed into bed.
I laid there for a bit and was just dropping off to sleep
when dad walked in. He said, 'Marie, are you not going
to put a drink out for father Christmas and a carrot for
Rudolf?'
I didn't have a clue what he was going on about. so I
followed him downstairs anyway. Just like he said we
put a mince pie on a plate with a glass of milk and a
carrot for Rudolf. We placed it all in front of the fire.
Dad said, 'Marie, if you have been a good girl, father
Christmas will come down the chimney and leave
presents under the tree for you; now come on you lot get
an early night or Santa won't come tonight.'
We went upstairs and all climbed into bed. Dad had
kissed Rosie on the cheek and then came over to me
He said, 'Can I have a kiss goodnight please? '
I leaned over and kissed him gentle on the cheek, 'Night
night Dad.'
He turned off the light and closed the door. Rosie and I
lay there talking about what we wanted to get if father
Christmas came. I had a really good sleep that night in
Rosie's lovely room.
In the morning, Katie and Kerry came rushing in.
Before I knew it they was dragging me out of bed. Half
asleep I was pulled out of the room into Mary and Dad's
room. Rosie started jumping on the bed shouting really
loud, 'Wake up wake up its Christmas.'

"Why"

I wanted to get her off, I thought she was going to get in to big trouble but dad and Mary just laughed and said, 'OK OK.

Now that everyone had been woken up by Katie and Kerry, we all went downstairs. Dad was right: Father Christmas did leave presents under the tree. He had also eaten the mince pie and the glass of milk was half empty and little nibbles taken out of the carrot.

I was confused. Dad told me why we put them out and that Father Christmas must of enjoy them

I stood there looking at all the presents, I didn't look at the tags.

I didn't think any of them would be for me - Alan was always telling me I was naughty. I couldn't believe it when Kerry handed me a present. I checked the tag and it had my name on it. I had the biggest smile in the world on my face. I looked over at Dad; he said, 'Open it then see what you've got, Marie. '

I couldn't stop smiling at the present in my hands. I ripped the paper off and saw a pretty pink dressing gown. Then I looked down at my feet and there was three more presents.

 I could of burst with excitement, I opened the rest: one was sweets, another was hair clips and hair bands, the best one was a spirograph.

 I asked Dad, 'Can I play with my toy please?

He laugh and said, 'Of course you can your the one who's been good.'

I took my spirograph up to the bedroom. I sat there nearly all day doing pretty patterns. As I sat their Rosie came in.

"Why"

'Why are you not playing downstairs?' she asked
I just told her, 'I like to be on my own.'
The truth was I was used to being alone and sent to my
bedroom. After a while I heard Dad say, 'Come down,
Marie, we are going to play games.'
We played musical chairs, Kerry missed once as she
went for a chair when the music stopped and fell on the
floor - we all laughed. Then we played sleeping lions;
Dad kept going around and tickling us so we moved
around and laughed.
Katie got up and shouted, 'That's not fair, Dad I was
winning until you tickled me. '
She was sulking; she just sat on a chair watching us play
in the end.
I could smell that Christmas dinner was cooking. It did
smelt lovely but still in my head I couldn't eat it. It was
like I was frightened to eat because of the fear of getting
fat .
When Mary told us all to wash our hands for dinner, I
didn't panic this time because I saw the napkins on the
table. I did eat some but only enough to keep a mouse
alive. I had lost loads of weight, but still all I saw was a
chubby girl in the mirror. After dinner I left the table and
I got rid of the food in my bag upstairs. I felt bad
because Mary was really nice and boy she could cook.
Everything which was on the table smelt lovely and
everyone had empty plates at the end of the meal.
When I went back downstairs, I was told that there was
another Christmas film on. That's when my dad told me,
'Marie, when the film finishes I will take you back home
as its a long drive.'

"Why"

I wanted to tell him I don't want to go; I just sat there
looking at the TV but not really watching it. I was really
sad; I had seen what life was suppose to be like and I
wanted it so bad.

"Why"

Chapter Eight

Well that's was it, I was going home i'd had so much fun and was going to miss everyone. while I was upstairs getting everything packed into my bag I was thinking. Why can Katie have this and I have Alan to put up with- did my dad not love me? I just didn't know the answer. I heard dad shout, 'Marie, are you ready? A tear rolled down my cheek. I picked up my bag and walked downstairs. Mary handed me a coat she said, 'Have this coat - it will be warmer. I hope you don't mind - its Kerry's old one.'

I took the coat. It looked almost brand new; it was bright red with fir around the hood. I hugged everyone and started to cry - I was crying because I was going to miss everyone, but mostly because I was going home.

It was only Me and Dad leaving the house to take me home, as it was starting to get dark and Mary wanted the girls to go to bed . As we drove along, I sat listening to the music; it didn't help my mood. My dad liked country music and It was all sad. I had stopped crying and must of fell asleep. I was woken with Dad saying 'Marie, you're home, sweetie wake up.'

Rubbing my eyes, I looked out the window - yes dad was right because there in front of me was home. We both got out the car and walked towards the house.

"Why"

I wanted so much for dad to say, I am telling your mum your coming to live with me. Even I knew that wasn't going to happen.

Mum must've seen us pull up, because the door opened before Dad had a chance to knock. I noticed and so did Dad that mum had a black eye. Dad asked, ' What have you done? '

Mum answered, 'I opened the kitchen door to quick and didn't get out of the way.' And she laughed.

Dad seemed to take that and said nothing more about it. We all went inside. mum asked, ' Do you want a cup of tea, Barry?'

Dad said, 'No thanks your OK, I want to get back as the roads are getting icy.'

Dad put my bag down and asked me for a cuddle.

He said, 'OK Marie, I have got to get back. I hope you had fun see you very soon. '

He kissed me on the cheek and headed for the front door. I waved at him until he was out of sight.

Mum yelled out, 'Shut that bloody door it's freezing. '

I walked into the front room where mum was sitting and asked, 'where is Alan?' I didn't care - I just didn't want him to just pop up without warning.

The TV and the Christmas decorations were missing, I noticed straight away as I had walked in but didn't say anything in front of Dad.

I asked mum again, 'Where is Alan? '

Mum said, 'He has gone to see his family; I don't know when he will be back.'

"Why"

I relaxed a bit when I heard mum's words. I asked,
'Mum are you OK?'

Mum said, 'I am fine and take your stuff upstairs and get
to bed.'

I picked up the bag and walked upstairs. As I was
walking up the stairs a cat was sitting on the top step; it
was black all over. Then on the landing I saw another
one - that was ginger I shouted, 'Mum some cats have
got in.'

Mum came to the bottom of the stairs and said, 'No they
are our cats.'

I smiled for the first time since I left Dad's house, the cat
fur was really soft. I walked into my bedroom and they
followed me. The black one jumped on my bed, that
night they both slept curled up with me on my bed.

Alan didn't return for a couple of days; it was nearly
time for me to go back to school. I soon knew when he
was back, because the shouting was the first sign - life
was back to it ugly self.

On the last day of the school holidays, I was sitting in
my room playing with my Spirograph, when Alan
walked into my room and told me, 'Get your coat on we
need to go out, I need some money.'

I wanted to tell him to go away, but I wasn't brave
enough so off I went and got ready.

We went around the streets looking in skips. Alan said,
'This is useless; lets go and see if there is any behind the
shops - they will be closed by the time we get there.'

It was starting to get dark and a lot colder; I just wanted
to go home.

"Why"

We turned off the road into the dark service road behind the shops.
There was only a small light shining above a door about half way along. Right in the corner at the bottom of the service road was a massive skip. As we got nearer I could see it was almost full with all sorts of junk and a mattress chucked on top. Alan lifted up the mattress to see what was underneath.
'Right, Marie, get in to the skip.' he said
 I really didn't want to because I had my nice red coat on. Just as Id managed to get myself in and stand up, Alan was climbing in behind me. Just then I felt his hands on my back pushing me hard, I fell face first onto the dirty damp mattress; It smelt disgusting - all I could smell was urine. Then Alan rolled me over and was on top of me, slapping me really hard round the face. He said, 'Keep fucking quite.'
I lay there with his heavy weight on me. He was hurting me because I was skin and bones. He pushed my trousers down, then his hands were between my legs grabbing at my knickers.
He hissed down my ear, 'Girl you need to eat more - you're too dam skinny.' In my head I was smiling.
 I was hoping and praying he was going to leave me alone. I could feel the freezing cold air on my half-naked body and the cold damp mattress underneath me. Putting his hand over my mouth he still continued to push inside me. I wanted to just disappear anywhere but there with him.

"Why"

After he finished, he told me 'Pull your clothes back on and get out of the skip.' I didn't want to leave. I thought that living in this skip was better than my life.

We walked home. As Alan had sold his bike for drink, Mum still made me go with him to report back to her. As we was walking home that night Alan repeated 'Why are you so skinny, girl ?'

I replied, 'I am not.'

He said, 'Yes you are. Don't worry, I will fix that.'

I didn't want him to fix anything; I just want him to go away and never return and leave me alone.

We reached home and mum was in her usual spot sitting on the sofa watching TV,I went upstairs and was glad it was bath night. So after they had theirs I got myself in. The water was stone cold but I was relieved; I could wash the stench of Alan and the smell of the mattress off me. Although I washed the smells and the mess off me I couldn't make the pain he left me or the question why disappear.

After I had got myself ready went to bed, I cried myself to sleep like I did almost every night. I didn't want my life anymore; I wanted a life like Katie's.

Its was the first day back at school. I still hadn't made any friends.

I was the smelly quite child of my class. I didn't try to make friends either, because I didn't want to get close to someone again and have to lose them. Most days went passed in a blur; I was mostly dreaming in my own little world, where I had a family that loved me.

"Why"

After being back at school for a few weeks Mum told me, 'You will have to be careful with the cats, because they are both going to have babies.'

I loved the cats - they was the only things in my life that seemed to love me. Most of the time the cats were up in my bedroom with me.

They both started to get really fat, After about nine weeks mum called me down as I was up in my room. I went into the dining room; there I watched with amazement at the cats giving birth. Between them they had thirteen little balls of fluff; they were so small but there mums where really good with them.

In a couple of weeks they where running around the dining room. Alan was always moaning about them getting under his feet. So mum made a pen to keep them in. I loved watching the kittens play with there cute little faces and soft meows.

The only trouble was they made a lot of mess; It was my job to clean it up before and after school.

I didn't mind clearing up there mess - it meant I could spend time holding and stroking them. The little pure white kitten was my favourite, it would always fall asleep on my lap while I was stoking it.

One morning I had got up for school; it must have been giro day. Alan as usual was at the bedroom window looking for the postman.

I got ready and left for school before the postman came. That day id got home from school, to find mum with cuts and bruises and the house smashed up.

I asked her, 'Where is Alan?'

"Why"

She said, 'He has taken most of the money and gone out
drinking again.'
 The horror that met me, when I went to say hello to the
cats, stopped me near the doorway. The cat's play pen
was smashed to bits,the walls splattered with blood, The
tiny little kittens bodies were scattered all over the
dining room. Tears streaming down my face. I went to
mum and asked, 'What happened to the kittens?'
Mum said, 'Alan kicked them, because he came back
drunk and wanted the rest of the money and I wouldn't
give him it.'
She added, 'They got under his feet and he said that you
spent too much time with them.'
I went back in the dining room, on my hands and knees
checking every ball of fluff for signs of life, hoping at
least one of them would still be alive, but not one - all of
them were lifeless.
Mum got up and joined me in the dining room; we
started to clean the kittens up. I came to the pure white
kitten,its tiny body broken and its fur red with blood.
We where both in the dining room and I let my emotions
get the better of me. I shouted really loud, 'Alan's a
fucking bully.'
Mum came over to where I was and slapped me round
the head   shouting, 'How dare you say that. Get out of
my sight and get to your room.' I got up and left mum to
it. She made me sick. Why she was always sticking up
for him? As I reach the top step I shouted, 'Mum where
are the mum cats?'

93

"Why"

Mum shouted, 'They were out at the time that Alan went mad.'

I was happy - at least they were OK. I went into my bedroom and opened my window and called them. They came straight away. I felt so sad for them; that night they both slept on my bed with me.

Alan didn't come back – he'd done a disappearing act for a couple of days. He came back three days later; it was Friday and I'd just got back from school. As I walked into the house I could hear them rowing. I just went straight up to my room to keep out of the way. While I was up there I could hear nearly every word they was saying. I heard mum say, 'Who the fuck is she then?,who do you go and see?' Alan said, 'I go and see my family in Cambridge.'

Mum replied, 'Why do you always go on your own ?' Alan said, 'Come with me then.'

Mum said, 'Ok, we will next time.' I rolled my eyes because I didn't want to go.

The next day mum came in my room, as I was waking up.

She said, 'Put something nice on as we are going to meet Alan's family.'

She looked happy and Alan wasn't drunk for a change. We all left and caught the bus; we were on the bus for ages and then we had to change buses. When we arrived in Cambridge Alan's brother was waiting for us in his car. When we got into the car he smelt just like Alan normal does, when he kicks off . He was driving really fast, I didn't like it but I just sat there quite, holding tight on to the door handle.

"Why"

We pulled up outside a house where a women was standing near the door.

'That's my sister at the door.' Alan told us.

We all got out of the car and walked up the path. Everyone seemed to be nice and we all sat down for dinner. I sneaked my dinner into trousers pocket, while nobody was looking. I nearly got caught a few times but nobody said anything. After dinner I went and flushed it down the toilet.

As we all sat there watching TV, everyone started drinking and the atmosphere got worst. Alan's sister and one of his brother's started to pick fun of me. Saying, 'God Alan do you not feed this girl.' His sister pinching my side hard, trying to find some fat.

The music started and was put on really loud. Alan ordered mum: 'Give me some money, Sue.'

Mum said, 'I've not got a lot; I spent most of it on bus fare to get here, Alan.'

He exploded ' We can't eat all my fucking sister's food and give nothing back. Lets buy some drink for everyone.'

Mum picked up her handbag and started to look for her purse; she pulled it out of her bag and said, 'Come on, Marie, you can keep me company.'

When we were both outside, the door was slammed in our faces.

All we heard was Alan saying, 'Right, you can fuck off home now.' And he started laughing.

His sister was at the window upstairs; she was throwing our clothes out of the window at us.

"Why"

Alan shouted, 'Thanks for the money, we will make sure we have a drink for you.' Mum opened her purse. There was nothing inside - all the money had been taken.

Mum shouted, 'You can't leave me out here at this time of night with no money and miles from home.'
Alan answered, 'Piss off now your boring me.'
We both walked away from the house; it was cold, dark and raining hard. Mum started crying when I asked 'What are we going to do, Mum?'
She said, 'I don't know Marie, I don't even know where we are. '
I said, 'Why don't we phone the police?'
She said ' I've got no money, remember.' Then mum thought of an idea she told me,
'Go to that door, knock and ask where we are and put the water works on.' so off I went.
When the door was answered the man said, 'Hello, can I help ? its very late - who are you?'
I said, 'Me and my mum have no money and we have been kicked out, we are lost and we are a long way from home.'
At that moment mum was beside me. She told the man what had happened and where we lived.
The man said, 'I can't take you home - that's a long way - but I can take you to the petrol station that is on the motorway, I will give you some money and hopefully you can get someone to give you a lift from there.'
Mum said, 'Thank you that will be a big help.'
The man said, 'Do you want to step in out of the rain while I get my coat and car keys?'

"Why"

His house was nice and warm, hall full of pictures of his family.

We got into his car; he was trying to make conversation with Mum but she was only giving him one word answers.

As we pulled into a petrol station he said, 'Sorry I can't help more; take this Thirty pounds - its all I have on me. I hope you get home safe.' He drove away. I watched the back of the car disappear from view.

So there was mum and me at a cold, windy petrol station on the edge of the motorway. I said, 'Now we have some money we can get a bus or something.'

Tucking the Thirty pounds into her purse she said, 'No way. I am keeping that - we are hitch hiking.' I looked at her in disbelief.

Mum grabbed my hand. We left the bright lights of the petrol station and headed out into the rain towards the motorway.

As we walked down the slip road and alongside of the motorway, Mum told me, 'Hold your thumb out.'

As we was walking along with only the car head lights to pierce the dark motorway as they passed us. As the lorries went passed there was a big gust of wind, driving the cold rain into my face.

My little legs were freezing, I was soaking wet. After walking in the dark for what seemed like ages, a car pulled over and the driver opened the window asking Mum, 'Where are you going?'

Mum said, 'We need to get back to Essex near the Dartford tunnel.'

"Why"

The women said, 'I can take you some of the way but I am not going all the way - will that help you ?'
 Mum said, 'Yes. Marie, get into the back of the car.'
 It was much warmer in the car and nice to get out of the rain. The women was really chatty and she handed me a bag of crisp. I didn't open them but it was nice of her. Mum didn't tell her what had happened with Alan, she just gave her a pack of lies.
With my head leaning on the car door I nearly fell asleep. After a while the women left the motorway and pulled over near a roundabout.
She said, 'Sorry I can't take you all the way home; I hope you get home soon.' Me and mum was out in the pouring rain again, with our thumbs out and walking onto another motorway; my legs were getting heavy and tired. A car pulled over in front of us. When we got level with the car a man poked his head out of the window.
He said, 'Where are you trying to get to, ladies?'
Mum said, 'Tilbury.'
He replied 'I am going through the tunnel - if I drop you off just before can you walk from there?'
Mum said, ' We can do its not far but I have no money on me to give you.'
The man said, 'Don't worry about that, Jump in.'
Just like the man said, he dropped us off just before the tunnel. The sky was getting lighter, the rain had stopped but I was still soaking wet and freezing cold. When we reached Tilbury, I started to recognise places from when I had been out with Alan.

"Why"

We arrived home. Mum said, 'Right get yourself to bed.' I got into bed and tried to warm myself up, my legs aching and red raw. I fell asleep as soon as my head touched the pillow.

"Why"

Chapter Nine

After a few weeks Alan hadn't returned, I actually started to let myself relax. As there was no rowing or night visits I was getting a good night's sleep. Mum was really strict but she was nothing compared to him. I really thought and hoped he wasn't coming back. All my hopes and dreams were shattered, when I was up in my room doing my homework. I heard the usual shouting, the sound track to my life. I knew straight away it was his voice and him hammering on the front door. After a short while the shouting and banging stopped.

I heard mum say, 'You can come in, but I don't want any trouble.'

Alan replied, 'I promise there will be no trouble.'

She unlocked the door and let him in, closing the front door shut. Mum shouted up the stairs, 'Marie come down, Alan has something for you.'

I reluctantly went downstairs and towards the laughter that was coming from the kitchen. Mum was standing waiting for the kettle to boil, while Alan was leaning on the frame of the back door smoking one of his roll ups.

Alan said, 'Here you are Marie, this is for you.'

It was a bag of sweets, I didn't want anything from him. As he handed them to me he said, 'I have missed you and your mum. Enjoy the sweets - you need fattening up.'

"Why"

I took them and asked, 'Can I go back to my room now and finish my homework please? '

Mum said, 'Yes, say thank you.'

Through gritted teeth I muttered, 'Thanks, Alan, for the sweets.'

I left them and walked back through the lounge towards the stairs. Lying on the coffee table in the middle of the room was a big bunch of flowers.

Under my breath I said, 'God, Mum, why are you so stupid.'

On getting back to my room I closed the door behind me and chucked the sweets on top of my cupboard.

Later that evening mum called me down to make the tea.

While I was in the kitchen making them their tea, Mum and Alan were all over each other kissing and cuddling. I Looked at them with everything crossed, hoping it would stop him coming into my room tonight. I thought maybe I was safe as he seemed all loved up with mum. That night I lay in bed looking at my bedroom door, I just couldn't seem to get off to sleep.

I heard mum and Alan giggling and laughing, as they came up the stairs and go into their bedroom. I must have relaxed enough to fall asleep. I woke with a start as I heard my bedroom door handle move. I just had the worst ever sickening feeling, in the pit of my stomach; I knew it was him coming to get me.

I lay there with my eyes squeezed tightly shut, hoping he would leave me alone if he thought I was asleep.

"Why"

No, he grabbed the covers, pulling them off me, straight away he was on top of me. Using his body weight to hold me down. He was being a lot rougher and forcing himself harder inside me .

After what felt like a lifetime, he had finished moving and moaning on me. He got off me and went over to the cupboard that the sweets were on.

Snatching them off the cupboard, he came back over to where I was sitting on the bed. With his nose touching mine, he said, 'What? not good enough for you, you little bastard?' Taking a sweet out of the bag, he pushed me on my back and forced it into my mouth. With his tobacco-stained fingers pinching my nose. I couldn't breathe, I started to choke.

He released my nose from his fingers. He just let out that laugh again.

Leaning towards me, he whispered in my ear, 'You will fucking eat, I like some meat on your bones.'

He left my bedroom closing the door behind him, leaving me crying and feeling sore and dirty. He had given mum flowers and me sweets but he was still the same sick, horrible beast.

From that night on, every mealtime he would sit right next to me. Watching me eat every mouthful of my food. Waiting to slap me hard round the head if I didn't eat what was in front of me.

When he was bringing my food from the kitchen to the dining room, he would purposely drop most of my food on the floor.

"Why"

 While he was bending down to pick it up and putting it back on my plate he would look at me with a big grin on his face, saying Sarcastically, ' Oops, sorry, Marie, I dropped your dinner.'
He would place the plate in front of me, watching me to make sure I was eating it.
Things turned even worse. It was one evening when mum had gone to bingo. He had my sandwich already made for me when I got home from school which seemed strange.
 I didn't have to eat it straight away, as I had my homework to do.
Then I heard him shout my name 'Marie, your mum's gone to bingo, come and have your tea.'
I got my night dress on and went downstairs. I was really hoping he'd forget to give me tea that night. But no luck as I walked into the dining room he was sitting at the table 'Come and sit here, Marie.' Tapping on the seat next to him.
 I looked down at the sandwich in front of me. It looked like it had chocolate spread in it, which I didn't mind.
 I didn't get many things like chocolate spread. So I picked up the sandwich and thought right let's get this down me, then I can go to bed and get out of Alan's way
 As I lifted the sandwich towards my mouth I looked at Alan.
He said, 'Go on, Marie, eat it.'

"Why"

Once the sandwich was under my nose there was a strong smell of shit. I knew exactly what was in the sandwich. A tear rolled down my cheek, knowing deep in my heart he was going to make me eat it.

I said, 'I am not hungry, Alan please can I leave it?' He grabbed the sandwich from me and forced it into my mouth.

I started to gag, with him shouting, 'Start eating your fucking food or this will be your dinner every day.' Just then I was sick all over the table, he pulled me off the chair.

Throwing me on the floor, he swung his leg back and kicked me full force in the stomach. I folded up into a ball as all the air left my body. He lifted my face off the floor by grabbing my hair.

'You're no good to me if your all skin and bone, so I want you to eat.' I didn't say a word I just looked at him and asking myself why.

He said, 'After you have cleaned your mess up, you can go to your room, but remember eat your food or you will get more sandwiches like that.'

When I finished cleaning up,I went upstairs and into the bathroom. I was sick again, until there was nothing left in my stomach.

I washed my mouth out and tried to get rid of the taste. Rinsing my mouth the best I could with just water, I couldn't stop gagging.

I finished in the bathroom and took myself to bed still gagging. I couldn't get what had just happened out of my head.

"Why"

Crying into my pillow I just didn't want to live any more. I hated everything about my life, Alan was controlling me and I just didn't know how to stop it.

Alan would sit watching me eat, forcing me to clear my plate every meal time. For a few months, he would always give me food he knew I didn't like. While watching me eat he would say, 'If you don't like eating that, then I will have to do you a special sandwich.' The thought of it would make me gag and I would force myself to eat what was in front of me.

In the end I didn't have any fight left in me. So whatever he gave me for dinner, I would eat it up as fast as I could. Just to get tea time over with - even if the food had been on the floor - I had given up, I was just a shell. I soon started to put weight on again. I hated the sight of myself in the mirror. I was so frustrated because I was powerless to stop what was happening to my life.

One evening mum was in the lounge, while Alan was sitting watching me eat my dinner. He said,'At the weekend I am going out to the industrial estate. Marie won't be able to get over the fences so I will go on my own.'

Mum answered. ' You mean you're off to see some tart.'

'I am going on my own, Sue.' he replied as he left the table and flew into the lounge.

While they were arguing, I went to the bin, took some of the rubbish out and tipped my dinner in. Putting the Rubbish back in, on top of the food and then just sat at the table with an empty plate.

"Why"

He returned into the kitchen and got a beer from the fridge.

He said, ' Wash up and get up to your room, Marie.'

The rowing went on for most of the night. I only knew it had stopped when he paid me a visit during the night.

The weekend came and Alan was up and out by the time I had got up. All day long mum was snapping and lashing out at me for nothing.

When Alan came back he was drunk and mum hit the roof.

She said, 'You said you was going to the industrial estate and you have been in the pub all day - where did you get the money from?'

Doing his best to stand up he said, 'I found a HIFI system in a skip and my mate bought it off me.'

Mum went mad, 'That's the last time you go out without her; at least she can keep an eye on you.'

I hated going out and spending all day with him - why did mum have to keep sending me, why couldn't she go?

So I still had to go out with Alan when he went looking for stuff. On one of these days out we had just left the house. He said 'Right, Marie, your back to your pretty weight again - we are going to see my friends again today.' My heart sank but what could I do?

I was a little girl and he was a big-built man; he was the boss. I though about making a run for it but he would catch up with me no problem then I would be in big trouble.

We was heading back to the house with the dirty nets up at the windows. With all the dirty men that liked hurting and using me like Alan did.

106

"Why"

I tried to walk as slow as I could, but this just made Alan mad. After a while we arrived. When we entered the house the smell of stale fags and sweat hit me. The man that opened the door to us, handed Alan some money. Patting me on the head and smiling at me with his toothless grin as he went up the stairs, he said, 'Alan, bring her up in a minute.'

I was taken upstairs being pulled every step by my hair. Taking me into the same room as before, he pushed me down with such force my feet left the floor. I ended up lying on the bed. Alan then grabbed me by my throat with both hands and said, 'Do as you're told; they can do what they like - they have paid for it.'

He pulled at my clothes, leaving me naked on the bed, closing the door behind him, throwing the room into darkness.

I wanted to get up off the bed and run away, but I heard loads of foot steps on the stairs. The bedroom door opened and about four men entered the room.

I could hear there belts clinking as they undid them. Their dirty cold hands started touching all over my seven year old body. One of them was pushing my legs apart, forcing himself inside me. My body arched in pain as I let out a scream. Another man was standing over my head forcing his thing into my mouth Making me gag. Then a voice in the dark said, 'I want my share.'

They both stopped only to be replaced by the other two men. They kept swapping around, using my young body like a lump of meat.

 Then it all stopped but they was still in the room.

"Why"

 I could hear them all moaning and started to feel warm
splashes all over my face and sore broken body, leaving
me sore and burning. I was a broken child and this was
my life and I hated it. I cried as I lay in the dark knowing
it wasn't going to change. Alan came back into the room
stinking of beer. He said, 'Clean yourself up.'
I jumped up and went to the bathroom, cleaning myself
up the best I could and as quickly as possible. I just
wanted to get out of this hell hole.
Tears still filling my eyes as I walked home. In my head
I was calling Alan all the names I knew -I wasn't stupid
or brave enough to say them out aloud.
Every car that went past, I wanted it to run up on to the
pavement and run him over - or better still run me over.
When we got home mum was sitting on the sofa; she had
a flannel on her head. I asked,'What is the matter, Mum?'
She said, 'I have got one of my bad headaches, Marie.
Can you get some of my tablets from the kitchen - I will
need them to help me sleep.'
I passed them to her and went up to my room to clean
myself with the cold water from the tank. Later that
night I was lying in bed with the cats on my feet,
wishing I had a tablet that I could take - I didn't want to
wake up and live my nightmare life anymore.

"Why"

Chapter Ten

At least there was some sunshine pouring back into my life. I was in the kitchen washing up, when there was a knock the door .

I was told to answer the door. Standing at the door was a plump grey haired old lady with little a bald old man.

The old lady said, 'Hello you must be Marie?'

Mum came to see who it was, then mum said, 'Marie, let your Nan and Grandad in.'

We all sat around the table; I sat there staring at my Nan and Grandad. Nan said to me, 'You have grown a lot since the last time I saw you , I think the last time was when you was playing in my back garden, you must have been about two.'

I didn't know I had a Nan and Grandad let alone what she was on about. Nan said, 'Your birthday must be coming up soon, Marie.'

I said, 'Yes, Nan, its soon.'

Nan asked Mum if I could go over and stay at hers some weekends. I was looking at mum with everything crossed waiting for her answer. Thankfully mum said, 'Yes that's fine with me.'I was over the moon. At least I wouldn't have to go out with Alan at the weekends.

Once they had gone I had to finish the washing up but for the first time in ages I had something to smile about.

"Why"

I was bursting with excitement when mum joined me in the kitchen, I couldn't hold my excitement in anymore. I had to know more about my Nan and Grandad.

I said, ' Mum I didn't know I had a Nan and Grandad.'
Trying her best to dampen my excitement mum snapped back, 'They are your dad's mum and dad.'
Wondering about her mum and dad I asked, 'What about your mum about dad?'
She said, 'They died before you was born, Marie. now can you stop asking questions, finish your chores and get to bed.'

The following Friday I was making my way home from school. As I got near the house I spotted a beige car with a brown roof parked outside our house. When I knocked on the door Nan answered it saying, 'We have been waiting for you, Marie,Would you like to come and stay with us for the weekend?'

The smile on my face must have said it all.
Nan said, 'Good, mum has made a weekend bag up for you; when Grandad has finishes his cup of tea we will go.'
From the lounge Grandad said, 'I am ready when you are Winifred.'
We said our goodbyes, Nan picked up my bag and we headed for the beige car. We headed out towards the countryside. Before to long Grandad said, 'Here we are.'
We pulled up next to a small cottage with a well kept front garden.

Me and Nan went inside to put the kettle on, while Grandad put the car in the garage. Nan gave me a tour of her garden, showing me Grandad's vegetable patch and all her fruit trees.

"Why"

Nan said, 'Shall we make some fruit pies tomorrow, Marie?'

I said, 'yes can we eat them as well Nan?'

She started laughing. ' No point making them if we are not going to eat them.'

We went back indoors and Grandad was asleep in the arm chair with His newspaper on his lap, my eyes drawn to his caterpillar like eyebrows. Nan give him a nudge and he woke up.

She said, 'We haven't seen Marie for ages and you nod off ,Frank. Frank you can entertain Marie while I go and make tea.'

Grandad folded up his newspaper and tucked it down beside him.

We sat chatting until Nan called me into the kitchen.

She said, 'Would you like a drink, Marie?'

She had her hands in a great big bowl, giving me directions to where everything was.

I was standing next to her filling up my cup with water when I asked, ' What are you doing nan?'

She said, 'I am making a meat pie. Do you want to help me?'

I said, 'What can I do?'

Looking at me over the top of her glasses she said, 'Wash your hands first then get yourself a pinny off the back door - you can roll out the pastry.'

She wrapped the pinny round me. 'Hang on, there's something missing.'

Dipping her finger in the flour she had poured over the work top,she dabbed it on my nose.'That's better - you look like a real baker now.' We finished making the pie and popped it in the oven.

"Why"

After dinner Nan got the snakes and ladders out while Grandad fell asleep in front of the TV. I started yawning. Nan made me a Horlicks and took me up to bed, sitting with me, telling me a story until I fell asleep. For the first time in my life there was someone who loved me.

When I got downstairs for breakfast, Nan was coming in from the garden with a big bowl of apples saying, 'These are for our apple pie that we are going to make later on.'

When the pie was all made Nan said 'We will have to walk down the the village shop and get some custard.'

On the way to the shop, Nan stopped and chatted to everyone that we bumped into, telling them who I was and that I was here all weekend.

On the way back from the shop we stopped in at her friend's house a few doors along from Nan's.

As we opened her front gate, a small black dog came running from the back of the house, tail wagging and barking like it was pleased to see us. Nan said 'That's Alice's dog Benson; we can take him for a walk around the lakes later if you like, Marie.'

I really didn't care what we did - I was just happy to be spending time with Nan and Grandad. Nan and Alice chatted, while I played in the garden with Benson.

When we arrived back at Nan's Grandad tried squirting us with the hose while he was washing his car. Grandad said, 'Do you want to help me wash the car, Marie?'

I said, ' Yes, but I can't reach the roof.'

He laughed ' I will do the roof if you do the sides, Marie.'

"Why"

Every time I went near the bucket of soapy water
Grandad would squirt Me - by the time we was finished
I was soaked.
For the rest of the evening, I was in the kitchen with Nan
making cup cakes.
The next morning after breakfast, we went along to
Alice's house to get Benson. Once we had his lead on
him, we headed out of the village down a small country
lane.
We came to a lake, a few people fishing and a couple
waterskiing.
We walked right to the other side of the lake. We sat on a
bench, letting Benson off the lead for a sniff about while
we had a cup cake each. We sat there in the warm
sunshine for a while.
Nan said, 'We best get back home, Marie, we need to
have lunch and then take you home.'
My heart sank, I had forgotten about home.
Praying it would be soon I asked, 'When can I come
back over Nan?'
Nan said, 'We will have to ask your mum, Marie.' We
finished our walk around the lake and went home.
While the lunch was cooking nan ran me a deep hot bath
with loads of bubbles. Nan popped her head around the
door. I jumped up out of the water and covered myself
up.
She said, ' You're OK, Marie, its only me - don't look so
worried. When you get out of there I will brush your hair
and help you get your things together.' I smiled at her
and lowered myself back into the bath.

"Why"

I looked like a prune by the time I got out of the bath.
Nan was sitting on my bed with a hair brush in her hand
waiting for me.

While she was brushing my hair, we talked about what
we was going to do the next time I came over and how
much she loved having me over to help her.

We all sat down to a roast chicken with all the trimmings
and Grandad's home grown vegetables.

I was eating as slowly as I could, to put off going home
for as long as I could. Unfortunately I couldn't put it off
for ever. Before long I was in the car heading back to my
nightmare.

When we arrived back home, Alan and Mum was sitting
in the lounge watching TV. After Mum had made a cup
of tea.

Nan and Mum sat chatting, while Alan just stared at the
TV.

Nan asked, ' Sue, could we have Marie over for tea one
night after school?'

Alan's head spun round to face them.

Mum said, 'Of course you can, Winnie, how about
Wednesday?'

Nan smiled. 'Ok we will pick her up straight from school
and have her back by half past seven.' I was so pleased
Mum had said yes.

I looked at Alan; I could tell by the look on his face, he
wasn't happy. Catching a glimpse of Alan with a face
like thunder, as I gave Nan and Grandad a massive hug
as they was leaving. I stood at the door waving at them
until they was out of sight.

"Why"

As soon as I closed the door Alan sent me straight to bed. I Lay in bed thinking about my fantastic weekend at Nan's.

I could hear Alan shouting, ' Why the fuck did you let her go over there again?'

Mum said, 'Because she is Marie's Nan, Alan.'

Alan said, 'Don't give me all that bollocks, sue. Don't expect me to do her chores while she's over there-she can do them when she gets back.' by the tone of his voice he was fuming, Mum trying to calm him down.

'Well I could hardly say no could I, Alan.'

The rowing went on for ages,I blocked it all out with my happy memories of my weekend and fell asleep.

Alan paid me the usual middle of the night visit.

He was rougher with me than ever before, leaving me burning and sore. After he had gone back in to his bed with Mum, I sat on my bed just wishing I could go and live with Nan and Grandad; Wednesday couldn't come quick enough.

All of Wednesday afternoon, I was looking out of the classroom window trying to spot Grandad's car. Nan and Grandad arrived just as the bell went. I ran across the playground as fast as my legs would carry me. Nan was standing at the school gate with her arms out holding bag of sweets. I jumped into her arms and she gave me the biggest hug I had ever had.

On the way to the car she handed me the sweets saying, 'Don't share them with grandad - they will play havoc with his false teeth.' we both roared laughing.

"Why"

We got to Nan's house. she said, ' Marie, we have to go
on an errand. In this village we all grow different things
and swap them with each other, so we have got to take
some of Grandad's potatoes over to the lady opposite.'
She packed a great big bag with the potatoes. We went
across to the lady's house and came back with a bag of
tomatoes and a lettuce.
Carrying the bags back nan started to get short of breath.
'I will need to take my spray when we get home.' she
puffed.
I panicked. 'What is that for nan?'
She said, ' I have got a poorly heart, Marie and the spray
helps look after it.'
We arrived back and Grandad was in the kitchen. I asked
him, 'Where is Nan's spray, Grandad, Nan needs it?'
He said, 'Its in her bag, Marie. that's the trouble with
your Nan: she is bloody stubborn.'
After nan had taken her spray and had a sit down for a
while she seemed to be ok. So she set about getting tea
made with my help. The evening passed in a flash and
before I knew it I was in the car heading home.
We pulled up outside my house and Nan came to the
door. Alan answered the door without a word to us, he
called Mum and turned back to the lounge.
Mum arrived at the door with a massive black eye.
Sounding shocked, nan asked, 'What have you done,
Sue?' Lying again Mum said, 'I walked into a cupboard
door, winnie.'
Nan ignored her answer and told mum more than asked:
'We will pick Marie up on Friday after school as its her
birthday next week.'

"Why"

Mum said, 'OK winnie.'

Nan hugged me and said, 'See you Friday poppet.'

I said, 'See you Friday Nan.' I couldn't wait.

As I was standing on the door step, waving bye to Nan and Grandad, Mum leaned over my shoulder' Come on in now, the washing up needs doing.'

I knew before I went into the house, Alan would be unhappy about me going to Nan's again. Passing him in the lounge I could feel his glare on me. He got up from the sofa and followed me into the kitchen. Grabbing the top of my arm, spinning me round, growling at me he said, 'I don't like you going to your Nan's all the time, I will have to find a way of stopping you.'

Fighting back my tears I asked, 'Why can't I go to Nan's?'.

He said, 'Your place is here and you are mine not your Nan's. Don't forget, if you tell her about our secret, she wouldn't believe you because she's old.' Running this thumb across his throat letting out his sick laugh, he stood at the kitchen door watching me wash up.

When the washing up was done, he barked, ' Now piss off to bed your getting on my nerves.'

That night the same as every night he came in to my bedroom to use and abuse my body. The whole time he was telling me, he hated my Nan and how she was a horrible old woman. After he had gone back to bed with mum, I tried to work out why he hated my Nan so much.

Friday morning, I was sitting having my breakfast before school. Alan was standing over me moaning about my weekend at Nan's.

"Why"

I wasn't taking much notice of him, until he walked
passed me and drove his boot into my back saying,
' Have a nice weekend, I will be waiting for you when
you get back.' I started crying with pain in my back.
He shouted, 'Shut up, you will have your mother down
here.'
As soon as he was out in the garden, I chucked the rest
of my breakfast into the bin and left for school.
During the day at school, my back was starting to get
stiff and a reminder of the pain every time I moved.
The bell that I had been waiting for sounded. I made my
way to the school gate, looking for Nan but I couldn't
see her. I started to think that Alan had stopped me going
with her for the weekend and she wasn't coming to pick
me up. When I got to the gate I looked up and down the
road. In the distance I spotted Grandad's car and Nan
walking towards me. I thought thank God for that as I
was smiling from ear to ear. I ran towards her just
wanting to get into Grandad's car and go. Just in case
Alan was going to appear from nowhere and stop me
going.
Once I was in the car and we was moving I relaxed. As
we passed the top of my road, Nan looking down it
towards my house.
She said, 'I don't know what it is but I just don't like
Alan.' Grandad just nodded.
Nan carried on, 'He never works, he is always rude - I
just don't like the way he looks at me.'
All the way back to Nan's she was talking about Alan
with Grandad just nodding.
After dinner Nan ran me a bath with loads of bubbles.

"Why"

She said, 'When you have had your bath, Marie, come downstairs and you can have your birthday presents.' She pulled the bathroom door shut as she left me to it. When I was undressed I looked at my back in the mirror. In the middle of my back was a round, dark purple bruise that Alan had left me with.

After my bath I joined Nan and Grandad in the lounge. On Nan's lap was two presents wrapped in birthday wrapping paper and on the table a glass of orange juice. Nan passed me the presents.She said 'happy birthday, Marie, you can open them now if you want to.' I ripped at the paper.

Grandad was laughing. 'You made short work of that, Marie.'

They had given me a pretty dress and a teddy bear.

Nan said, ' You will have to go to bed soon, Marie, we have got a busy day in the kitchen tomorrow.'

I asked, 'What are we making Nan?'

She said, 'How about making some fruit pies, cakes and maybe some jams. Maybe we can make Grandad pop if we make enough.' I got into bed; as soon as Nan turned out the light I was asleep.

The weekend went in a flash and I was back at home. It became the norm for Nan to pick me up from school. Wednesdays for tea and on Fridays for the weekend. Nan would spoil me rotten, always buying me little presents for no reason.

We would always bake something to take up to the lakes while we was walking Benson, always stopping at the bench at the end watching the men fish while we had our snack.

"Why"

Nan was getting slower on our trips to the lakes and would always use her spray when we got to the bench. We parked ourselves on the bench one Sunday morning. After Nan got her breath back she said, 'Would you like to come and stay with me for a couple of weeks, when your school breaks up for the summer, Marie?'
I replied, 'I would love to Nan.'
She said, 'When we take you home later I will arrange it all with your mum.'
All the way back to Nan's, I was thinking all that time I was going to have with my lovely nan and be away from Alan. We arrived back at Nan's; she took the calender down off the wall.
Flicking over a couple of pages she wrote Marie coming for two weeks. I didn't want to get my hopes up to much - I didn't think mum would let me stay that long, being sure Alan wouldn't like it and try to stop it happening.
Nan and Grandad came into the house when they dropped me off.
Straight away Nan said, ' Sue, we would love to have Marie over for a couple of weeks in the summer holidays.'
Mum shot a look at Alan, but she said, ' Ok if its not to much trouble for you.'
Nan replied, 'No, we love having Marie around the place .'
Nan stayed chatting with mum a bit longer about my holiday at hers.
Alan sat staring at the TV - it was written all over his face: Alan hated the fact that he couldn't seem to stop me going to Nan's.

"Why"

He let me know every chance he got that he wasn't happy about it, giving me a slap or a kick when ever he could; the more he kicked and hit me the more determined I was to go to Nan's.

One night I was woken by the sound of my bedroom door opening. I knew he was going to force himself inside me.

He was moving around on top of me with his hand over my mouth, again leaving me sore and burning just like every other night. I lay on my bed thinking about telling Nan when I was with her for a couple of weeks.

Would she believe me or would it make it all this worse? The following Weekend came; me and Nan was in the kitchen.

Nan asked, 'Marie, would you pop down the shop to get some sugar for me, please?'

I said, 'Yes, Nan, is that all you need?'

She said, 'I think so. If you pass me my purse will sort you some money out.' She rummaged in her purse ' I don't have any change - you will have to take a ten pound note.'

I took off my apron and slipped the money into my pocket and wondered off to the village shop. I bought the sugar and made my way back, stopping to chat to a few of Nan's friends.

When I got to Nan's garden gate, taking the change out of my pocket to hand it to her when I got in, I only had the coins in my hand - the five pound note was missing.

"Why"

I recovered my steps back to the shop but I couldn't find the five pound note. With my eyes scanning the ground I was starting to panic. Nan is going to go mad and I was in for a good beating that I had lost her money. I got back to Nan's house and the fiver was still missing. My heart pounding as I got to the back door. Pushing the door open I burst into tears. Nan said, 'What is the matter Marie?'

Sobbing and scared, I said, 'I have lost the five pound note that was in your change, Nan. I have been back to the shop to see if I can find it.'

She put her arms round me saying, 'Its OK, Marie, these things happen.'

I said, 'I didn't do it on purpose, nan,' begging her to believe me. Nan said, 'Its OK, I know you didn't, I believe you Marie. Come on dry your tears then we can finish the cakes.'

Nan believed me. I had nothing to lose by telling her about Alan. I made up my mind, I was going to tell her on the first day of my long stay at Nan's in a few weeks time.

I was soon back home with Alan and mum, I couldn't wait to be back at Nan's.

I was into my last week at school before the summer holidays, getting more excited about going to Nan's with each day that passed. When I got home from school Mum was standing at the door. I could see she had been crying by her red eyes. I thought that she and Alan had been rowing again and the house was going to be smashed up.

As I passed her she said, 'Go in the lounge and sit down, Marie.'

"Why"

I said, 'why?'
As I sat down mum said, 'I have got something to tell
you, Marie, your Nan has passed away.' I burst into
tears. My world had just fallen apart taking all my hope
with it.

I know I hadn't known her long, she was such a lovely
lady. She was so nice to me and I loved her with all my
heart. I even loved her more than my mum.

After a few weeks of snide remarks form Alan about not
being able to go to Nan's anymore, he went off to see
his family.

After he left the house Mum told me, 'Marie, you need
to have a bath tonight.'

I said, 'Why, Mum its not bath night?'

Mum said, 'Tomorrow we are going to say bye to your
Nan.'

In the morning mum had laid out all black clothes on my
bed.

Auntie Dot came to take us to Nan's funeral. We went to
the big church near the lakes in Nan's village. We parked
up near the church; everyone that lived in the village
was there in black. Standing outside the church was Dad
and Mary with Katie. Dad give me a big hug when he
saw me; he seemed really upset. I felt really bad,
because I thought to myself that I wouldn't be sad if I
didn't see my own mum again. I didn't want to not ever
see Nan again though -the thought of it filled me with
sadness. Everyone went inside the church; Grandad was
crying. There was a wooden box and mum said, 'Nan is
in there and she going for a long sleep.' I wanted to run
up and shout take me with you, Nan.

123

"Why"

After the service we all drove to a cemetery and Nan was lowered into the ground. we all went back to Nan's house. I went up to the room where I was going to stay. The whole place smelt of nan. That's when I started to cry again and I hugged the pillow and said, 'Bye, Nan, I will miss you. I love you loads always.'

Dad walked in and sat next to me and said, 'Nan will always be looking down on you, she loved you so much.' Hearing my Dad's words made me smile.

After everyone said their byes Dad gave me and Mum a lift home.

When he dropped us off I asked, 'Dad, when can I come to yours again? '

He said, 'soon sweetheart.'

He drove away, and after that day I didn't see dad for a long time.

A few nights after Nan's funeral Alan returned. That night he came and used my young body for his sick pleasure. After he left, the anger growing inside me I said, 'I cant take this anymore.' I left my room. I crept downstairs and went to the cupboard where Mum's tablets were. Taking the bottle back up to my room I sat on my bed with a glass of water in my hand. I started to swallow the tablets, crying and saying I am coming with you Nan I want to sleep now. After I had taken around twenty tablets I started to feel sleepy. I smiled as I lay on my bed drifting in and out of sleep, I saw Nan's face; I popped more tablets into my mouth, nan started shouting wake up wake up, Marie, wake up, you will win.

"Why"

The next thing I knew, mum was in front of me sticking her fingers down my throat. I was sick everywhere.

A strange man In a uniform came into my bedroom. He lead me down the stairs and towards the ambulance outside with its lights flashing.

I must of drifted off again, as the first thing I knew after this was a nurse waking me up with some food. Mum turned up on her own and hugged me, whispering in my ear, ' Your making me look like a bad mum, you wait till I get you home.'

A doctor came round and said, 'Marie, we are going to send you to speak to someone,'

Mum piped up, 'Its probably because she's missing her Nan so much, her Nan has only just passed away I will keep an eye on her.'

The doctor said, 'OK you can go home.'

We walked out the hospital and got on the bus to go home. when we reached home I was sent up to my room. After a while of me being home mum came up to my room. 'Marie, you are a stupid girl, why did you do it ?'

I said, 'I don't know. ' I remembered the excuse mum had used in the hospital so I added, 'I miss Nan loads.'

Mum said, 'Do it again and you wont need tablets next time because I will kill you myself.'

Mum left my room. I looked around my room and noticed my record player wasn't in my room. I shouted to Mum as I could hear her in her room,'Mum, where is my record player? '

Mum said, 'Alan threw it out - you don't deserve it.'

I didn't take tablets again. My throat killed me for days after.

"Why"

I found something that helped instead: I started to pull my hair out.
 I couldn't stop eating, because of Alan forcing me to eat. So maybe if I was ugly in another way, maybe that would stop him. I was just an eight year old girl trying to stop all the pain and misery in her life.

"Why"

Chapter Eleven

Most of the time I had to wear a head scarf, to cover up
the bald patches I left by pulling my hair out in big
clumps. A letter had arrived from the hospital for my
follow-up appointment. Mum ignored the letter and
never took me back to the hospital. There was no let up
in the mental and physical abuse from Alan.
Mum sent me out with him when he went looking in
skips.
When he wasn't having much luck in finding anything, I
was told I had to make it worth his while for coming out.
So on the way home he would find somewhere quiet,
making me get on my knees in front of him.
After a few trips out he found loads of fishing gear.
Being pleased with his find we headed straight home.
When arrived home Mum was in the kitchen. ' What the
hell have you got there, Alan?'
' its fishing gear,' he replied
Mum said, 'What do you want that for? You don't go
fishing?'
He said, 'well I do now.'
mum said, 'That's just another excuse for you to go and
see your tart, Alan.'Thinking to myself please don't make
me go fishing with him.
The normal row exploded about Alan going on his own.
I was gutted when mum said, ' If your going fishing you
will have to take Marie with you.'

"Why"

I Wanted to scream can't you see what he's doing, Mum. Can't you see, he starts the rows by saying he wants to go on his own, knowing you will send me and then he gets me alone to do what ever his sick mind wants.

Now he had his fishing gear it was either going round the skips or fishing. Most of the time we went fishing; we walked miles to lakes or rivers. When we got there, he would take his time to look for a place to fish where no one could see us, so he could have his dirty sordid way with me.

My life was an endless string of abuse. From being a slave that was forced to eat, to my body being used by Alan and his sick friends.

Why was it, whenever someone nice came into my life, something went wrong and I lost them.

Alan was always using me like I was his toy to play with, whenever he wanted to. Every time he was done with using me, he would tell me, 'You are a worthless, dirty girl that no one loved; if you disappeared no one would miss you.'

He didn't have to tell me all these things, I knew them all already. He had abused me so much, I didn't know who I was. I was just a robot everyone else controlled.

I was about ten years old, when Alan was going out fishing and I was sent with him. When the light started to fade he began to pack up his gear. He said, 'Right, come on, we need to get home.'

"Why"

Walking across the fields on the way home, he pointed to some brushes and said, 'Get in there.' I knew what was coming.

Don't ask me why, because I wouldn't be able to tell you why, but I got into the brushes Alan said, 'Right lay down and hurry up, we can't be late home as your mum will wonder why.'

Just as he was going to put all his weight on me I brought my knee up, with as much force as I could and caught him right between his legs. He rolled off, holding himself.

He then grabbed hold of me and punched me in the stomach, saying, 'You're a little bitch. Don't worry, you might not get it now, but I will get you back for this.' Then he said, 'Right, get out of here and get home.'

I was happy because I found a way that he would leave me alone. I was also shitting myself. I didn't know what he was going to give me. My mind was running overtime while we walked home, thinking of what he was going to do to me.

When we got home I was just sent straight to bed. He told mum I had been naughty; like always she believed every lie that came out of his mouth.

I don't know why but I think I would've rather him kick the hell out of me because this not knowing was worst. For the next few days I was jumping at every sight or sound of Alan, I was walking around on egg shells, thinking is it now that I was going to pay for kicking him. It was nearly a week and it was a night when mum was going to bingo.

"Why"

I was being left with Alan. Mum had just left; I heard the front door close behind her.

Alan called me down. I went down to the lounge where Alan was.

He had pulled the sofa out into the middle of the room. Holding a glass of water in his hand he shouted, 'Come here.'

I walked over to where he was standing. He grabbed my hair and spat in my face, then he said, 'Right, get in,' pointing to the cupboard under the stairs.

He said, 'Sit in there, I hope you like your new bedroom.' I just looked at him

He added, ' And you better keep quite, because if Mum hears you I will stab her and then stab you.' I stepped in and sat on the floor among the boxes and junk. He placed the glass of water on the floor in front of me.

He said, 'I have put a pen mark at the level of the water; if you touch one drop of it I will know, and I will break every bone in your body.'

He closed the cupboard door, throwing the cupboard in to darkness.

The only light I had was coming through a small crack at the top of the door.

I could hear him pushing the sofa across the floor, then a thud as the sofa hit the cupboard door.

I sat in the pitch black wiping his old stale fag spit off my face, wondering what was he going to do with me now.

My eyes adjusted to the dark; I could just make out the glass on the floor in front of me.

"Why"

I sat there for ages thinking any minute now, I will hear
him move the sofa and he will let me out just before
mum gets home. I was wrong. I heard mum come home
from bingo. I could just about hear there voices over the
TV. 'Is Marie in bed?' Mum asked
Alan said, 'Her dad came round and she has gone to stay
with him for a week.' They must have gone in to the
kitchen as there voices faded.
All of a sudden the light coming through the crack
disappeared. Then I heard Mum and Alan's footsteps on
the stairs above me as they went up to bed. I tried to
stretch my legs out the best I could in the cramped
cupboard. The longer the night went on the colder it got.
My feet like blocks of ice. I sat shivering in my thin
nightie, all night listening to the house creak and moan. I
was bursting for a wee; I couldn't hold on any longer and
I wet myself.
The faint morning light was coming through the crack. I
could hear the faint sounds of movement upstairs. My
legs were aching and my bum numb in the cramped
cupboard. I tried to moving them without knocking
something over and making a noise.
It must have been pay day; the shouting started from
upstairs. Then two sets of heavy footsteps above me, I
tried moving again while there was lots of noise. They
carried on rowing about the money.
Mum was crying as things started getting smashed. The
crashing and smashing stopped with Mum screaming,
'Come back, Alan.' The front door slammed making the
whole house shake.

"Why"

A few seconds later the door was slammed shut again. I sat for a while listening for the slightest sound. It looked like I was the only one in the house. I stood up the best I could; hunched over I pushed at the door with everything I had. I kept on trying and trying but it wouldn't move an inch.

 I slumped myself back down on the floor; I was so tired I fell asleep sitting up.

Waking up to the sound of someone walking up the stairs, I was starving hungry, and the smell of dinner cooking made it worst.

Covering my stomach with my hands to muffle the sound of it rumbling, just in case anyone heard. I heard the front door slam again and Alan slurring his words, Mum pleading with him not to start any trouble.

The rest of that evening, I sat listening to them watching the TV, waiting for him to explode.

Night had descended again bringing with it the freezing cold. I hated nights and the dark at the best of times. All night I sat looking at the crack in the door, waiting for the day light to appear.

I was so thirsty by the time morning came, my tongue sticking to the top of my mouth it was so dry. Staring at the glass of water in front of me, I couldn't help myself.

 I dipped my finger into the water and licked the water from my finger. The water felt so good in my mouth. I just wanted to pick the glass up and drink the whole glass.

A few times I reached out to the glass. I wasn't brave enough to drink the water.

"Why"

I sat in the cupboard all day listening to mum and Alan, sitting on the sofa on the other side of the door watching TV. My belly rumbling was getting louder and the stomach cramps getting worst.

As I leaned forward to ease the pain in my stomach, I broke wind.

I shook with fear, as I thought mum would hear and then Alan would stab us.

Mum did hear – she said, ' Alan was that you ?'

He said, 'yeah sorry.'

I was waiting for all the screaming and shouting to start with Alan going berserk, it never came but the fear stayed with me.

Mum Shouted, 'I am off to bingo, will see you later, Alan.'

Alan yelled 'OK.'

The house fell silent,until I heard him moving the sofa away from the cupboard door. The door swung open. He grunted, 'Get out.'

I crawled out, using the arm of the sofa to get to me feet. He bent down and picked up the glass of water, checking the level, letting out that laugh again.

I had to lean on the sofa because my legs couldn't hold me on their own.

He grabbed my arm and spun me round, forcing me to bend over the arm of the sofa. He lifted my night dress and pulled down my knickers, pushing his way inside me making me burn and sore more than ever before.

When he had finished abusing me, I though he was going to tell me to clean myself up and let me out of the cupboard.

"Why"

Instead he told me, 'Stay there, I will get you something to eat.'

He came back with a slice of bread and handed it to me. The hunger took over. I snatched it from him and stuffed it in to my mouth. The taste of it was vile and I spat it out: he had pissed on the bread.

He said, 'Ok, you wasteful little bitch - you can stay in there for another two days.' He shoved me back into the cupboard, slamming the door behind me. He said, 'Don't forget, if your mum hears you, I will kill the pair of you.' I spent my time in the cupboard thinking of Nan: in my dreams she was there with me. I think even now if she wasn't I would of cracked up.

After a few more days he opened the door again. He told me, 'Your mum is out go and have a bath.'

I ran the bath and washed myself as quick as I could, worried he would come up and put me under the water again. Before I had finished drying myself, he burst into the bathroom and ordered me to get on my knees in front of him. Making me suck his man thing, warning me, 'You will know about it and you will spent more time in the cupboard, if you didn't tell mum that you have been at your dad's and you had a wonderful time.'

I couldn't believe mum didn't care where I was. I could have been anywhere because she couldn't of checked that I was at Dad's or she would've found out.

When mum arrived home from wherever she had been she said, 'Hello stranger did you have fun?' I could feel Alan's eyes burning into me. I said, 'Yeah, it was great.'

"Why"

She didn't even notice that I had less hair and weight on my bones. It felt like my mum walked round with her hands over her eyes and her fingers in her ears.
while in the cupboard I was still pulling my hair out, so much so when I came out I had patches of hair missing. I started to wear my scarf all the time to hide my head. Mum asked, 'Why are you always wearing that scarf?'
I fobbed her off. 'Its the fashion, Mum.' She took that as my answer and never mentioned it again.
I went up to my room and cried as I felt so alone. Did no one care? Was this my life? What had I done so wrong? Feeling alone most of the time, sore and hurting, either from the beating that I had got for something or the sexual abuse. The treatment I was giving myself by pulling my hair out was hurting. But it helped because by this time, crying just seemed not enough to give me peace.
My body was changing as well. I started to get cramps in my stomach.
I put it down to what Alan and the men in the dirty house were doing to me.
The only thing in the house that show me love was the cats. I wasn't really allowed them in my room. One day I was at my bedroom window, calling the cats up onto the kitchen roof. Just as one of them was coming in the open window, I heard someone coming up the stairs.
I quickly closed the window, catching the cat's tail in the window; the cat sank its teeth into my finger I felt so bad that I had hurt the cat. My finger ballooned up really big and Mum actually noticed.

"Why"

So I had to tell her what had happened, and instead of sorting out my bitten finger, she lashed out with a hard slap and sent me to bed without tea. My finger was really throbbing, but the cat were fine.

I was so glad about this I loved the cats and it was the last thing I wanted to do was cause them pain.

A few weeks after this, mum started to pack up our stuff around the house, just like she did when we moved to this prison I lived in now.

So I asked, ' Are we moving again, Mum?'
She said, 'Yes, Marie, we are going back to Basildon where you went to school with sally.'
When I got to my room after hearing this, I was so happy I danced around my room. After I had finished my dance I went down. I had forgotten to ask when.
Mum was in the kitchen 'Mum when are we moving?'
Mum said, 'After Christmas. '
I asked, 'Will I go to my old school with sally ?'
Mum said, 'No, Marie, you will be going to a different school for a little while then after the summer you will be going to big school.'
I went back up to my room and was a bit worried about this big school - what if sally wasn't at this school? On the other hand I was still happy, I would be away from the dirty house, with them men who used my poor little body for their sick pleasure .
School broke up for Christmas, I never looked forward to Christmas anymore. It was just drinking, rowing and beatings, so what was there to look forward to. But this Christmas was a bit different.

136

"Why"

Two days before Mum said, 'Marie, Alan's family are
coming to us for Christmas, so you will have to give up
your bed, you will have to make up a bed on the floor in
your room; Alan's sister will be sleep in your bed.'I
wasn't happy, the last time me and mum saw them we
was thrown out, into the rain, along away from home
with no money - and they liked to drink like Alan.
They turned up. There were four of them: Alan's sister,
brother and two other men. Alan's brother slept in the
room where Alan he kept his weights; the other two men
slept on the sofa and chairs put together.
 At first everyone was being nice to each other.
 I was mostly up in my room, I felt safe up there.
 But on Christmas eve night they all started to drink and
that's when all hell broke loose. Mum told them that they
would have to leave if they wanted to drink. She was
just told to shut up and they carried on.
Mum wouldn't give in. I sat upstairs listening to it all.
Then I heard a massive crash. Alan sister shouting, 'God
sake, Alan are you stupid call an ambulance.'
I crept down. I saw mum had been pushed out of the
front room window.
I opened the front door. In the front garden lay mum
with blood all over her face. Alan just standing at the
window, drinking his beer.
I went to where mum lay. As I knelt down beside Mum
trying to help her to sit up, the street was filled with blue
flashing lights as the police and an ambulance turned up.
They attended to mum; she wasn't that badly hurt after
all.

"Why"

After they had patched her up, the policeman asked, 'What had happened?'
Mum said, 'I was a bit drunk and fell towards the window and went through it.'
The policeman made a few notes and handed my mum a card.
' If you remember what actually happened ring us.' The police and ambulance left.
I was ordered to get out of Alan's sight. So I did just that but that wasn't then end of the rowing. About an hour after all that happened they all left the house leaving me home alone. I sat there rather glad they had left me in peace.
Soon after they had left I heard the door go again. I didn't go and see who it was because I didn't really care.
I soon found out. Alan walked into my room having trouble keep upright. Falling all over the place, he walked over to me, shouting, 'Get on your knees.'
When I was on my knees he grabbed my head, nearly pulling my hair out, Saying 'I forgot to give you your present.'
I felt him in my mouth, pushing really hard, making me gag tears rolling down my cheeks. After he had finished with me he left me in a heap on the floor. I didn't cry anymore because no one cared anyway.
His family stayed until new year's eve and every night there was rows. On boxing day night, the two blokes had a really big fight in the front room, smashing the TV.

"Why"

Alan's sister was vile. she would spit in my face when she walked passed me. I was glad when they left. Alan went with them and was up there with them for two weeks. The house was quite and felt safe when Alan wasn't there.

But sadly he returned just three days before I had to start back at school. The front window had been boarding up and stayed like that for a while. The council told Mum she had to pay for it but Mum refused.

In the end mum had to pay because if she didn't they wouldn't let us move. I was glad Mum paid because I just wanted to leave this house and this town.

"Why"

Chapter Twelve

I didn't go back to school after the Christmas holidays, As we were moving again in a few days. Mum said it wasn't worth buying me a uniform, for a school that I was only going to for a few days. I stayed home and helped mum pack the house up. The day before we moved Alan said, 'I want to go out looking for skips.' Mum moaned, 'We had enough stuff to take back to Basildon.'

Alan said, 'I am only looking that's all.'

I knew what was coming next. 'Well you can take Marie with you.' Mums word sent a chill down my spine. Somehow I knew we wasn't going to be looking for skips.

Soon as we was out of the house. He broke the news we was going to see his friends. On the long walk to the dirty house, I was having flash backs of my previous visits. We turned into the road and there it was, this run down dump of a house.

The feeling in the pit of my stomach made me feel sick. Alan holding my arm, he lead me up the path and knocked on the door.

The same toothless man answered the door, he never said a word just nodded in the direction of the inside of the house. Standing in the hallway, the toothless man handed Alan some money.

"Why"

Quickly counting the money, Alan said, ' There's not enough here - I want at least half again.'
The toothless man went into the lounge and came back with more money.
'Its all there mate, you can take her up - the room is ready.'
Pushing me towards the stairs, Alan said, ' Get up there.'
I was taken into the same room as before.
Alan leant down to my face. 'Get undressed and lay down, they have paid good money - give them what they want or else.' He watched me undress then he left the room.
This time it was different: he left the light on and the door open.
A group of men came into the room; the first man bent me over and forced himself inside me. At the same time a man forced his thing into my mouth, another put his fingers up my bum. I thought I was going to die on the spot the pain ripped through my body.
I was turned over; one of the men was on top of me pushing inside me again. Another was standing at the edge of the bed playing with himself.
White sticky stuff was squirted all over my face, Alan came back in and force himself in me.
I noticed a man in the corner of the room, taking photos and playing with himself.
They didn't just use their things inside me, I had bottles and a buzzing plastic object which looked like there things used on me. After what seemed like ages, it all stopped. My whole body was sore and shacking, my legs wouldn't work.

"Why"

Alan grabbed me and pulled me to my feet, pushing me forwards towards the door. I fell to the floor; all the men laughed.

Alan shouted, 'Go and clean yourself up, you dirty bitch.'

Whilst in the bathroom I looked into the mirror, wishing I could climb threw it. Maybe life was better on the other side than the hell I was trapped in.

I found some toilet paper on the floor; I wiped myself the best I could.

Still feeling dirty I left the bathroom and went down the stairs.

Alan was sitting in the front room with everyone else. He finished his drink and ordered me: ' Say bye to my friends - you won't be see them anymore.'

I said in a quite voice: 'Bye,' as I looked at me feet.

Me and Alan left, but just before we got home he stopped me. 'Right, now listen to me, tell Mum we couldn't find anything worth having today.'I just nodded.

Mum was packing up the last few bits when we arrived home; as usual Alan made up some lies about me being naughty and sent me straight to bed.

I used some of the water in the tank and an old t-shirt; starting to scrub at my skin I scrubbed so hard I made my skin bleed, I just couldn't get rid of the smell.

I sat on my bed, I was bleeding from inside me and my body hurt every time I moved.

I must've of drifted off to sleep, The next thing I knew mum came in my room. 'Get dressed, Marie and pack the last of your things up, the van will be here soon.'

"Why"

Without a word I pulled myself to my feet and went to the bathroom.

I was shocked when I wiped myself as I was still bleeding. I felt sick. I thought maybe I was going to die. I rolled up some toilet paper to stop the blood from going on my knickers. I got dressed I was scared; they were rough with me but it had always stopped by the morning.

After I had finished with the stuff in my room, I went down stairs and had to help with moving stuff out to the van. I wasn't sad this time, I was happy to be leaving and happy to be moving back to the town where sally lived. The house we pulled up outside, looked like the house we lived in before. When the van door was opened, I rushed out and begged mum to open the front door as I needed the toilet. I ran up the stairs and sat with relief, then was scared out of my mind as I was still bleeding. The paper was covered in blood .

I put more toilet paper in my knickers and and went back down stairs.

I wanted to run up to mum and tell her I think that I am dying, but I knew better too. When we got everything off the van, Mum told me that we were going to walk down to the chip shop for dinner. Mum asked for fish and chip for her and pie and chips for Alan.

I was told I was only having chips - Mum said she didn't have much money left but added that I wouldn't like the other stuff they sold.

I didn't moan, I don't know why mum said anything - I was feeling lucky that I was getting chips.

"Why"

When mum said about dinner I thought, that it would only be their dinner from the chip shop, and I would have a sandwich as that was what normally happened. Me and mum walked back to the house; it wasn't far so we were back before the chips got cold. I was sent up to my room with my bag and mum and Alan sat on boxes in the the front room.

As I was sitting eating my dinner I felt like I was wetting myself. I didn't get up straight away, I finished my chips first. Screwing up the paper and putting it in the black bin bag, and took myself off to the bathroom.

I pulled my trousers down, I was shaking with fear, when I saw the amount of blood. It had gone right through the paper and my knickers and all over my trousers.

I cried out loud forgetting myself that Mum and Alan would hear.

Mum did hear me before long she was knocking at the door.

Mum said, 'Open the door.' I did as I was told.

When mum saw the blood I said, 'Mum I think I am dying.'

Mum laughed. 'No, Marie, your getting older, this will happen every four weeks for a week, every lady gets them.'

I said, 'so I am ok?' Mum said, 'yes you're OK. wait there, I will get something for you.'

Alan appeared at the top of the stairs. 'What is all the noise for?'

Mum said, 'Marie thinks she's dying. I've told her its normal for women to bleed.'

"Why"

Then mum returned and handed me this long pad; Mum told me that they are used for this thing. Mum went back downstairs laughing. As she went I was still confused. In some ways I was happy that I wasn't going to die but in other ways I hated my life.

Mum was right about the bleeding stopping after a week. Again we settled into our new house, back in Basildon and I started at a new junior school. I was only going to be there until the summer.

But I wish the abuse Alan gave me would stop but there was no let up... until around my twelfth birthday, he left me alone for a few weeks.

Until the night visits started again, I would tuck the covers right under me, making me sweating hot. I used all my body weight to hide under the covers the best I could. Lying there wrapped in my bed covers for protection, I would hear the click of my bedroom door handle, then my bed covers being pulled at.

It didn't matter how hard I held onto them, it was pointless. He would always give a hard yank and the warm bed covers would come flying off. Alan would cover my mouth, with his hand and take his sick pleasure out on my body ,leaving me lying there half naked, sore and feeling dirty. This happened nearly every night. Most nights when he left I would cry and speak to my Nan, begging her to come and get me but she never came.

The summer holidays were almost upon us.

"Why"

 Everyone in my class was getting excited about going
up the secondary school after the holidays. Mum had
got my uniform and equipment from one of her friends,
as her daughter had just left school and didn't need
them . I wasn't chubby anymore and most of the uniform
swamped me. I had to wear a belt with the skirt and roll
the sleeves up in the jumper.
I was still pulling out my hair. Mum took me to the
doctors.
The doctor said it was a skin condition and they would
need to do some tests. Mum was happy with the answer
that the doctor gave her and it was left at that and I
wasn't taken back for the tests.
So wearing the uniform and my head scarf, we walked
to the secondary school and into the office.
Mum told the lady about my scarf saying I had to wear it
because of a medical condition. When I was booked in
mum left and the teacher took me to my first class.
The teacher got everyone to say hi to me and then told
me to take my seat.
I looked around at everyone hoping to see my friend
Sally - would I even recognise her now? I had change
in looks maybe sally had too.
At lunch I sat in the Massive hall and had my dinner.
I got free school meals because Mum and Alan was on
benefits.
When I was finished I walked out to the playground.
Parking myself on a bench and watched the kids play. It
was scary as there was big kids at the school and they
called us the new ones.

"Why"

We had science after lunch which was one of my
favourites. After getting lost in the huge school building
I eventually found the classroom where I had to be. I
entered the classroom and took a seat at the back of the
class.
During the lesson a girl kept looking around at me.
When I caught her eye she smiled at me. I smiled back
wondering who she was.
When the bell rang for home time, I packed up my
things and headed out into the playground.
As I went out the gate, I saw the girl from my science
class again. This time she was calling out to me. 'Wait.'
 I stopped and waited for her to catch up, I didn't know
her but she seemed friendly. After being at my last
schools with no friends I waited for her. When she
reached me she was laughing. 'You don't remember me -
I am hurt.' as she put her hand on her chest.
I replied, 'No sorry, I don't know you.' Again she said,
'You don't remember? me I am deeply hurt.'
 I asked, 'What's your name ?'
She said, 'Guess.'
 I said, 'I am really sorry but I don't remember you.'
Then she said, 'Its sally.'
As her name came out of her mouth she flung her arms
around me. After we let each other go, we started to
walk home.
I had to walk past sally's home to get home myself sally
said, 'Come in and say hi to my mum.'
I said, 'I had better get home, I don't want to be late. '

"Why"

We said our byes and arranged that I would knock for
her in the morning. I walked home with the biggest
smile that day. When I got home, I told mum how my
day had been and that sally was at school. Totally
ignoring me she said, 'There is housework for you to do
before you go to bed.'
Even mum couldn't make me sad that night. Lying in
bed that night I tried really hard to fall asleep. I couldn't
sleep so I got myself out of bed and went to the window.
Looking out watching the sky turn from blue to black,
I lost track of time. I heard Mum and Alan coming up
the stairs going to bed themselves. I ran to my bed,
kicking the bed post letting out a moan.
My door opened Mum came storming in. 'What are you
doing out of bed? you should be asleep.'
Before I could answer she lifted her foot and removed
her slipper, taking her anger out on my back with her
slipper shouting, 'You're supposed to be asleep.' she left
slamming the door behind her.
I could feel the pain in my back, where the slipper had
landed on my skin, burning and sore, I laid down and
got comfortable the best I could, squeezing my eyes
closed, eventually falling asleep. Until Alan came in.
Awoken by the usual feeling of the covers being pulled
off me, I braced myself for what was coming my way.
Tonight was very different. Holding me down with his
body weight, he pressed something mental and cold
against my throat. He said, 'Make any sound and I will
cut your throat, then I will go and cut your Mum's
throat.'

148

"Why"

I lay there as still as I could, while Alan took his sick pleasure out on my body. Taking his body weight off me and releasing the knife from my throat, he left.

Like I said that night was different: this time the white liquid wasn't all over me; there was no sign of it. I pulled the covers back over me, rolling myself into a ball. I lay there until I finally fell asleep.

The morning came and I got myself ready for school. When I was wiping myself after going to the toilet, I noticed the white sticky liquid had come from inside me. I washed myself, rubbing so hard I made myself raw down below trying to feel cleaner.

I left the house after my breakfast and walked to sally's house.

I knocked and the door was opened by her mum. As soon as she saw me she hugged me. I was right back wishing that she was my mum, she was such a nice lady. She let me in; Sally was sitting in the lounge watching TV.

When she saw me she got up and started to get her shoes and coat on.

When she was ready she said, 'Come on, mate, lets go. '

Just as we was going out the front door Sally asked if she could have some money for the tuck shop.

Her mum opened her purse and gave her a fifty pence she turned to me.' There you go, Marie, one for you as well.' I couldn't believe she had just given me money, I couldn't thank her enough.

Me and sally left the house and walked to school. From that day I knocked for Sally every morning.

149

"Why"

We played with each other at break time. I had my
happiness back when I was at school, I Just wish home
life could be different. But no, the house we lived in had
a big garden. so Alan built a shed out of old doors and
bits of scrap wood and started to keep pigeons again.
He wasn't very good at building - when he was finished
the shed looked like it could fall down at any minute.
Then he had a go at making a fish pond that looked like
just a hole in the ground more than a fish pond.
Alan never went to a shop to buy his fish: he would
walk the streets at night, with a bucket and net. He
would look through the cracks in garden fences.
If he could see a pond he would climb over into the
garden and take the fish from the pond.
As usual when I was off school mum would make me go
with him. One night we walked right across town to the
park. Finding a gap in the fence he slipped himself
through,telling me to follow.
As we walked in to the darkness of the deserted park
towards the pond.
I was thinking, any second now he is going to push me
into a bush and force himself on me. We reached the
pond and he started to move his net through the water.
Whispering to me, 'Dip the bucket in the pond and fill it
up.'
I moved slightly away from him, just in case he decided
to try and push me in and hold me under the water.
Lifting the heavy bucket of water out of the pond, some
of the water splashed out on to the surface of the pond.

"Why"

He came racing over punching my arm.' Be fucking
quite, the park keeper's house is just over there.'
'sorry.' I whispered
He said,' You will be if he comes out of his house and
catches us.'
Snatching the bucket from me he carried on fishing.
As he was kneeling down trying to get his net as far into
the pond as he could, the though came into my head:
push him in and run. But where would I run to? I
wouldn't find that gap in the fence. I would be trapped in
a pitch black park with him hunting me down.
The urge to push him in was getting stronger. Holding
my breath, I shuffled slowly towards him trying not to
make a sound. Just as I was about the place my hands on
his back and use all my body weight to shove him in, he
turned his head ' what you creeping round for?'
Thinking on my feet I said, ' Haven't you caught any
yet?'
He replied, ' Just a few small ones, the net isn't long
enough to reach the bigger one's.'
We moved around the pond to try and catch more fish.
Eventually he said, 'I have got a good fish in the net.'
tipping it into the bucket.
He added, ' Right, we have got what we came for, lets
go.'
Making our way back to the gap in the fence, he grabbed
me dragging me behind a bush. He said,'Get down on
your knees. You didn't catch any fish so you are going to
have to make it worth my while bringing you,' getting
his thing out and pushing it into my mouth. The hatred
for mum building inside me.

"Why"

If she trusted Alan more, maybe I wouldn't have to go out with him all the time. I wasn't able to stop him from doing anything he wanted to me.

I did think what's the point of having a life. I was just a child slave with no voice and no choice, but to do what I was told. Because of all the rows about money, Mum would send me shopping. She would give me a ten pound note and shopping list with about forty pounds worth on. If I forgot anything or got caught I was in for a beating.

One Saturday afternoon I was walking out of the supermarket with the shopping, when I felt a hand grabbing me on my shoulder.

I thought I had been caught, but when I turned round I got the shock of my life: it was my dad standing there. I hadn't seen him in ages. He walked home with me. When we got into the road before my road, Dad stopped at a house he said, 'This is my house, Marie.'

A smile came right across my face and he hugged me. He said, 'Pop round when you like, I am sure your mum won't mind, its only me and Katie that live here - I am not with Mary anymore.'

I said, 'Ok I will ask her if I can come round.' I couldn't stop smiling

I waved bye and carried on my way; I was home in two minutes. When I walked into the house I told mum that I had seen Dad, telling her where he lived and that he'd said I could go round. she said nothing about it; Mum seemed not to care but I did.

"Why"

Life seemed to be getting better. We had only been back in this town for a couple of months: I had my best friend back and now my dad .

"Why"

Chapter Thirteen

The only good part of my life was school. The rest of My life didn't get better - it got much worse. A couple weeks after I had seen dad in town, I asked mum, 'Can I go round to see dad at the weekend?'
With her face full of anger she snapped, 'No you can't.'
Fighting back the tears, I said, 'Why not?'
She raised her voice again ' Because Alan said, you're not going to start going round there all the time like you did with your Nan, so don't ask again.' Dad never came round to get me either.
I would often sit in my room looking out of my window, thinking if those houses weren't there in the way, I would be able to at least see my dad's house.
The abuse from Alan was still happening. My breast were growing as my body was changing. At night he would always have a knife pressing up against my throat while he touched and used my body. Sometimes he would press so hard it left a mark, but Mum never noticed.
She didn't take any notice when I started being sick all the time. I couldn't keep anything down, It was worse in the morning and would ease as the day went on. Just the smell of food cooking would make me feel sick.
This went on for a few months; even though I hadn't eaten much I was putting weight on.
On one of the Alan's night visits, He punch me in the stomach for no reason.

"Why"

I doubled over in pain. He said, 'That should sort it.'
He left me lying on the bed holding my stomach.
The following morning, just as I got on to the stairs to
go down, Alan came behind me. I heard him say, 'Lets
make sure.'
Before I could work out what he was going on about, I
felt his foot land hard in the middle of my back. I didn't
have time to grab onto anything and down I went, hitting
my head and then everything went black.
   When I woke I was in hospital, I had a cut on my head
with a massive lump. My stomach was sore and
cramping.
A nurse told me that they was just keeping an eye on
me for twenty four hours, then I would be allowed
home.
When I got home I was told to get myself to bed. I took
my self to the toilet before bed.
Just as I did a big blood - looking lump came from
inside me. I just thought id started my women's week
and the pain was bruising from the fall down the stairs.
So I put a pad on but I had to keep taking myself to the
toilet to clean myself up.
For some reason I was bleeding a lot and in a lot of pain.
I didn't tell Mum because I thought I knew what was
happening to me - I was wrong. Years later I knew
exactly what was happening to me.
Alan had got me pregnant and then threw me down the
stairs to get rid of the problem, keeping his disgusting
secret quite. For a few day after that I was sore and my
stomach cramping.

"Why"

When I was better I was sent back to school, what a
relief to get back. Even if I wasn't very bright I still
enjoyed school and I loved my time with Sally.
My birthday was coming up. I asked if I could have sally
round for tea; As usual Mum flatly refused.
Nevertheless, Sally still bought me a lovely top to wear
for my birthday. It had a lovely sparkly cat on the front.
Just after I had got home from school there was a knock
at the door.
Mum called me, 'Marie, it's for you.'
Dad was standing on the door step when I got to the
door. He gave me a stereo and some money. He said, '
Get yourself something nice with that.'
I gave him a hug and said, 'Thank you, Dad.'
I think dad wanted to stay a bit longer, but as mum
hadn't invited him in he said he was busy and had to go.
As soon as the front door was closed mum snatched the
money for my hand.
She said, 'If you want to eat the food then you can buy
the food once in awhile.' that was the last I saw of my
birthday money.
The rows were still going on between Mum and Alan,
mostly about money. Often the rows would end, with
Mum having new bruises or cuts and something from
the house would be missing.
One evening just before Mum was going to bingo
Alan asked, ' Have you ever won anything at bingo?'
She said, ' No ,Alan. I have come close a few times.'
He commented, 'You must be the unluckiest woman in
the world, Sue - you always go to bingo but never win.'

"Why"

 I was in the kitchen listening to them getting louder,
thinking about the money the man had given us when
we had been kicked out of Alan's sister's house. She
must have won at bingo before and kept the money to
herself. They kept on rowing until all hell broke loose in
the lounge. Alan set about smashing up the house
looking for Mum's hidden money Shouting, 'If you have
money I want it - where is it?'
Mum screamed, 'The only money I have is for my books
tonight.'
Then I heard a crack and mum started yelling, 'Stop.'
He said, ' You're not going to bingo tonight. I am having
that money.'
All the shouting stopped as I went into the lounge. Mum
was on her knees with her hand over her eye and Alan
was nowhere to be seen.
When I got home the following day, Alan was sitting in
the lounge drinking. To stay out of his way I went up
into my bedroom.
The stereo that my dad had brought round for me was
missing. I shouted down to find out where it was.
I knew it was stupid but I only wanted to know. Alan
came running up the stairs and grabbed me by the throat
Shouting 'I took your bloody stereo; what are you going
to do about it?'
I kicked him by mistake because I couldn't breathe. He
dropped me to the floor, kicking me all over my body. I
heard him leave the house, with mum shouting after
him.
Mum soon returned without him, I was hoping he had
gone up to his family, but not tonight.

"Why"

In the early hours of the morning he returned, beating
Mum up and crashing out on the sofa. The next day
mum wasn't there in the morning. Alan was sitting on the
sofa. When I reached downstairs he told me, 'you're not
going to school today.'
 I didn't asks why, then he got up, grabbed me by the
arm, dragging me out into the garden and down to the
bird's shed.
 When we got there he opened the shed door, pushing
me inside he said, 'Do you like your new bedroom ?'
I looked round at the birds - they were flapping and
flying everywhere.
Alan walked toward the door and stepped out. He turned
back to me and said, 'Enjoy and you better be quite
because if your mum hears you, when you come out you
can clean up her blood.'
I stood there not knowing what to do, looking around at
the shed that was made from old doors and bits of rotten
wood.
I was so upset, I tried to be good but for some reason I
was always being told off.
 Mum returned home a bit later on. I heard her out in the
garden speaking to Alan while he was having a fag. I
heard him say that I was staying at my dad's for a few
days. That's when my heart sank; last time I was put
under the stairs he had said the same thing.
At that point I knew I would be in here for a while. I also
knew mum wouldn't check with Dad as she didn't last
time. She would never come down to the shed because
she hated the birds.

"Why"

The birds settled down because I wasn't moving and scaring them. I tried to find a clean spot on the bird poo covered floor but it was hard. Feeling the air temperature drop as the day light started to fade, I started to shiver - I was only wearing my school t-shirt and skirt that I had put on ready for school. Now I was stuck in birds shed. The wind was picking up and making the sides of the shed rattle and bang. Then it started to rain hard, with the wind driving the rain through the gaps in the walls. The rain water pouring through the roof... it didn't matter where I stood - I was getting wet.

The smell from the birds was really strong and was making my stomach churn. In one of the corners was a dead bird rotting. I didn't sleep at all that night.

Morning was dawning, my legs aching because I was standing up in the same spot all night. When I am alone in these situations I would talk to my Nan a lot because it gave me a little comfort.

It had been light for a few hours when Alan came down to the shed. Hearing him shout to mum that he was feeding the animals. He opened the door and entered the shed.

He looked at me and made the action, with his hand across his throat like he had a knife.

I looked down at my feet and backed away from him.
He laughed and threw some bread on the floor.

Saying, 'If you're hungry here is your breakfast - eat and enjoy.' He left locking the door and walked away, I was starving hungry but I would rather go without.

"Why"

I was just glad he had given me the choice whether to
eat or not . With the nights coming and going, I had been
out there for three days. Each morning giving me bread
to eat from the floor.
On the last morning in the shed, he came down with the
bread. Picking a slice of bread up that he had just thrown
down. He said, 'You must be hungry by now, Marie.'
Gripping my jaw he forced the bread into my mouth.
He left straight after, so I spat it out, Every day was
getting worst in there. Why couldn't my mum bump into
my dad or Dad come round then Alan would get caught
out. But I didn't have that sort of luck.
I stank to high heaven, my clothes covered in bird
droppings.
It was at night when I heard foot steps on the garden
path and a key unlocking the door. Alan came in. 'Right,
get yourself indoors and wash your clothes in the sink
and hang them up in the airing cupboard.'
As I walked towards him he punched me hard in the
stomach. 'That's just in case you're thinking about telling
mum that you haven't been to your dad's.'
 Mum was out at bingo again with her friend. I found out
that when Alan beat her up, it was round her friend she
would go. She never took me and I would always be left
in Alan's hands. Why did she never take me with her?
She'd leave me with a man that was capable of hurting
people and a bully. Did she not care what happened to
me at home or did she only look out for herself?

"Why"

I became an empty shell not talking and staying in my
room when I could; I was like a robot taking orders.
At school I was a completely different person; I would
put a front on. Because I didn't want people to hate me at
school. It worked because I had made friends and got on
well in my lessons, although I was never top of the class.
I never did P.E, because most of the time I had bruises
on my body.
So I would get a letter from Alan to excuse me from
taking part.
The only problem was my friends like to smoke. I tried
it one day down the bottom of the school field.
While others kept watch for teachers, I put the fag in my
mouth and had a drag - it nearly made me sick.
When I got used to it I was ok and I enjoyed it. Sally
tried it once, she didn't like it the taste; it made her feel
sick, so she never tried it again. But she still came down
the field with the rest of us.
One day one of the girls was using her lighter and
getting pieces of grass and setting them alight. She
dropped the grass and it set fire to the field because the
grass was so dry.
We all ran away as fast as we could; there was about ten
of us running in all directions.
The fire engines came and put the fire out.
We were never found out, but the fireman came into the
school and questioned us about it. We all kept our
mouths shut so they couldn't do anyone for it. My
friends were always asking if I was coming out to play
after school.

"Why"

I told them my mum didn't like me playing out.
One day when we was walking to school, one of my
friends came up with the idea of not going to school,
even sally said let's not go in.
So we didn't go in; we made our way to the park with a
boarded up building. We broke in to the building when it
started to rain.
I enjoyed that day so much; I felt normal. Me and sally
shared our friend's lunch as we didn't have anything to
eat because we had hot dinners.
After that day we didn't go in to school much. Sally and
me would get money off her mum most days and use this
to get something to eat.
We only went in to school to get marked into the
register, then hopped over the fence and went over the
park.
I knew I would be in real trouble, if I got caught but I
wasn't allowed out to play, so I took the chance. There
was a boy that took a liking to me but I wasn't interested,
I didn't like anyone touching me.
I knew this fun could never last. one day I was made to
feel really small. We were all over the park smoking and
drinking, just hanging out when we were supposed to be
at school.
Alan came walking through the park; before I knew it he
was behind me. He dragged me all the way back to
school by my hair. When I got home that night he beat
me black and blue. My friends came round to make sure
I was Ok. They were sent on their way; Mum told me to
tell them not to knock again.

"Why"

I didn't see them for a few days as I wasn't allowed because the state of me after he had beaten me to a pulp. I was kept off school until the bruising and swelling had gone.

When I did go back, my friends asked if I got into a lot of trouble. I said just grounded and the usual.

I told them my mum didn't like them because she thought they was a bad influence on me. They laughed, but agreed they wouldn't knock if it would get me into trouble. We knocked it on the head for a bit and went into school everyday, until the heat died down. After a few weeks we were back skipping school again . I liked school, but I craved the fun we had as well.

We came up with the idea of jumping on a bus and going to another town. So Me and Sally saved the money her mum gave us to use as bus fare.

When we had saved enough, we got our mark in the register and hopped over the fence.

We all caught the bus to Southend, Sally brought some clothes for me to change into. As we walked around the shops I was helping myself to music tapes, sweets, make - up or want ever I fancied having.

I was good at shop lifting – I had been taking things from shops for years because that's how I had to get Mum's shopping.

After we had gone to Southend once, we did it a couple of times because we wouldn't get caught by our parents. They would be at work back in Basildon so it was safer. But it did take awhile to save the money.

So when we didn't have the money we would go over the park, keeping our eyes open.

"Why"

We would climb into the building, so even if someone walked through, they wouldn't see us.

But again it couldn't last; the school sent a letter to Mum telling her that I had missed school. I got another good beating for this. After the bruising had gone down, I was taken to school and picked up by one of them. The only time I saw my friends was at school.

My time at home felt like being in a prison, spending most of my time in my bedroom. I didn't have a lot in my room, just a cupboard with my clothes in - not that I had a lot of them. There was my bed and a table that wobbled when I lent on it to draw. There wasn't any carpet on the floor, just cold bare floor boards. I wasn't allowed to have toys or any posters to brighten up my room. The only things I was allowed to have was pens and paper. That was about it my in my room, It never got decorated. It just had tatty old wallpaper that was covered in footballs.

Every now and then I had have a stereo or a TV but they were always disappearing.

Alan would sell them. Not that I was allowed to use them when they was in my room anyway - I don't know why they were ever given to me.

It was just before my fourteenth birthday and the Easter holidays were coming up and I was dreading it - being stuck at home with Mum and Alan for two weeks.

On the last day before the holidays, Mum picked me up from school.

I was shocked when mum announced, 'We are going to a campsite for a holiday next week.'

I said, 'where are we going ?'

"Why"

She said, 'One of my friends owns a caravan at Walton and has let us have it for a week at a good price. There is a swimming pool and loads of other things to do there.' That made me happy because now I could swim as I had been taught at school.

For the first time in a long time I had something to look forward to. Mum packed a suitcase and we all walked down to the bus stop.

After spending most of the day on buses we arrived at the campsite.

We walked passed rows and rows of caravans until we found our one. The campsite had a clubhouse, which had bands playing at night time.

While Alan and mum watched the entertainment, I was allowed to play with the other kids. During the day, I was given some freedom and allowed to the adventure playground. I became friendly with one girl - she was so lucky, her parents gave her whatever she wanted. I had a great time for the first couple of days.

Halfway through the holiday, me, Mum and Alan went to the beach. I was getting bored playing with the sand, so I asked if I could go for a swim in the sea . Mum allowed me, but Alan followed me in to the water.

I swam to the end of the pier. I looked round to find out where Alan was. I couldn't see him amongst all the other people bobbing about in the sea, so I just lay on my back and floated, looking up at the sky. The sun shone down on me; it was a lovely and peaceful. All of a sudden I felt something pulling me under the water.

"Why"

It didn't matter how hard I kicked I couldn't get to the
surface. Then I saw Alan face in front of me. I managed
to get my head above water and take a deep breath.
Then he pushed me under again, holding me down
swallowing loads of water. I really thought he was
going to keep me under until I was dead.
Mum couldn't see us - she probably thought we was
messing around. I was fighting for my breath; he let out
that laugh and let me go.
I got myself back to the beach as fast as I could. From
that day I have not been able to swim.
That night when me and mum was on our own in the
caravan getting ready to go to the club house, I was in
my bedroom getting dressed, when I heard the caravan
door open.
I stayed in the room, when mum started shouting: 'Alan
your not drinking anymore on this holiday.'
Alan replied, 'Fuck off, I will do what I like when I like.'
Mum never said another word; she just walked out of the
caravan, leaving me there with him. A chill went down
my spine and my stomach knotted up.
Here I was trapped in a small room with Alan drunk. I
couldn't believe Mum had left me again with him in that
state again.
I sat there listening to him staggering around and
knocking things over. The whole caravan shook as he fell
into the bedroom wall. I thought he was coming through
it. Then I heard him banging on the door, as he was
trying to get hold of the door handle. He yanked at the
door almost yanking it off its hinges.

"Why"

Leaning on the wall he slurred, ' Get up off the bed.' I
stood up not knowing what was coming.
Alan said, 'Take your clothes off.'
I pulled at my clothes, doing it as slowly as I could,
hoping he would get bored, but no I was stood there
naked trying to cover my body with my hands. He
lunged nearer to me; I could smell his stale breath he was
so close.
Grabbing my face, he started to fondle my breasts and
kiss me, the taste and smell was sickening. Before he had
time to do anything else, the door of the caravan opened.
He stopped and walked out of the room , leaving me
frightened and naked.
Looking down at my breasts, I hated them - I just wanted
to cut them off.
The relief when I heard mum's voice, as I knew he
wouldn't come back into my room with Mum there...
I got dressed again, while they were shouting and
hollering at each other.
After the caravan door slammed shut, it all went quiet.
Was I alone with him again?
I was sitting on my bed looking at the door handle,
waiting for it to move.
I couldn't hear a sound from inside the caravan. Was he
there or had he fallen asleep drunk? I stayed in there
until it was almost dark, plucking up the courage to open
my bedroom door. I edged towards the door, opening it
as quietly as I could, peering through the crack in the
door into the nearly dark caravan, checking to see if
anyone was there.

"Why"

They had both gone, leaving me alone in the caravan. The rest of the holiday I was walking on egg shells, waiting for him to find or make the slightest excuse to kick off. For once I was happy to get home; the holiday was nothing I thought it was going to be.

"Why"

Charter Fourteen

When we got home after the holiday, life didn't change. I was still the slave and the house punch bag. why didn't Mum ever stand up for me?

Soon after we had got back, me Mum and Alan were doing our usual thing: Mum and Alan downstairs and me up in my room, when there was a knock at the door.

Mum called out, ' Can you get the door, Marie, I am busy at the moment.'

I ran down and opened the door. In front of me there was a young man standing there. He said, ' Hi Marie.'

I said, ' Wait there a minute.' And closed the door.

I must of come across really rude but I didn't have a clue who he was. I went and got mum to come to the door. When she opened the door the young man said, 'Hi Mum.'

Mum said, 'You better come in.'

With me following, she led him into the lounge. Mum said to Alan, 'This is my son Chris.'

Alan said, 'Hello.' fixing his eyes back on the TV.

Turning to me she said, 'Go and make your brother a cup of tea.'

It confused me more, I didn't remember this young man.

Mum started quizzing him: 'What you doing in Basildon?'

Chris said, ' My foster mum has moved here - we live up near the park just up the road.'

'Oh right.' Mum nodded

' Do you know where dad lives, Mum?' asked Chris

Alan shot a look in Mum's direction - nervously she said ' No.'

"Why"

Alan piped up: ' Marie does, she has been there before.'
With Alan's eyes glued to me I told Chris where Dad
lived. Chris made his goodbyes and left.
I wanted to ask mum all about him,but I didn't - she
probably wouldn't have told me anyway. so I took
myself up to my prison cell of a bedroom, well that's
what it felt like.
It was back to school again. Mum and Alan had got lazy
about taking me to school, so I was allowed to go on my
own, I made a bee line and knocked for Sally.
The look of shock and surprise on her face was a picture,
when she saw me standing at her door.
On our way to school she asked, 'Did you have a good
holiday?'
Lying through my teeth,' Yes I had a great time, in the
clubhouse and swimming in the sea. What about your
holiday?'
She said, 'We went camping again, we went to a massive
campsite with a pool slide and a massive amusement
arcade.'
I added, 'There was an arcade on our site but it wasn't
that big so I only went in there once.'
I felt bad, because what she was saying was probably all
true and I was lying .
Sally asked, 'How come you're walking to school on
your own, Marie?'
Smiling I replied, ' My mum is still in bed and running
late.'
We reached school and we stayed there all day. A couple
of my friends jumped over the fence but I was too scared
to.

"Why"

Chris started visiting at least once a week. On one of his visits we were all sat in the lounge.

Chris said, ' I managed to find where Dad lives; I normally go and see him when I leave here.' Mum just nodded and he added ' Its my eighteenth birthday soon and Dad's throwing me a party at his house. Dad said you are all invited.'

As Alan huffed and left the room mum replied, 'That's nice of him.'

Mum changed the subject and Chris's party wasn't mentioned again.

I was hoping that mum would at least let me go, even if her and Alan didn't want to.

On the night of Chris's party, I did my chores and took myself up into my room. I sat at my window, looking at the houses that blocked my view of Dad's house, wishing I was there having fun with everyone else.

Chris popped round a few days after his birthday party. 'Why didn't you all come to my eighteenth?'

Mum said, 'Sorry but we was busy that night.' Which was a complete lie.

While her and Chris chatted, I was wondering why Dad hadn't come and got me. I suppose I had been forgotten as usual.

It felt like I was invisible. Katie was living with Dad and Dad held a party for Chris - what about me?

Why was I always left out on the good things but always remember first for the bad things? Did no one care about me? The only person that had showed they cared was my Nan and I had lost her.

"Why"

The weather was warming up, so Alan started his fishing up again. I had to go with him; sometimes Mum came as well. Most of the time it was just me and him. He would leave me alone, until we was all packed up and getting ready to go home.

He would find a bush or long grass or long corn to take me into and abuse me.

One day we had been at the lake from early morning until it got dark.

I was bored out of my brains - there was nothing for me to do but just sit.

I dreaded it, when he started to pack up his fishing gear. He smiled at me as we started to walk back across the field.

I was struggling to carry the big box which he sat on while fishing.

Walking in front of him, he kicked the back of my legs knocking me to the ground.

With the weight of the box, I hit the ground like a sack of spuds, my trousers soaked and covered in mud.

I looked up at him; he pointed towards an opening in a bush.'Get in there and hurry up.' he said

I got myself to my feet, with him right behind me and went towards the bush. Crouching over to get into the bush with Alan telling me to hurry up again, I placed the box on the ground, I stood there watching Alan get in.

I wanted to run, but I was frozen to the spot. He pushed me with such force, I ended up on the floor again. He told me: 'Take your trousers and knickers off.' Pulling at them, I was getting caked in more mud.

"Why"

Once I was naked from the waist down, he started undoing his trousers.

I closed my eyes and braced myself for what was coming. I could feel his hand forcing its way up my top. With the other hand on my legs as he grabbed and pulled them apart. I tried to take myself somewhere else, anywhere but there with him. I could feel the cold soft ground under me, my top soaking up the water like a sponge.

Then I felt him push hard into me, with all his weight on top of me. Then he stopped and climbed off me, he stood up and done up his trousers. I didn't move, I always waited for him to tell me to get up.

He pulled his foot up in the air and brought it down into my stomach. All the air left my body as I doubled over in pain.

He shouted, 'Get yourself fucking dressed, you dirty girl.'

I pulled myself to my feet and got dressed , pushing as much mud off my clothes as I could.

When we got home that day, Mum let rip at me because I was covered in mud. After she was done with beating me, she sent me to bed with nothing to eat.

I often sat on my bed, when sent there being accused of doing something wrong that I hadn't done.

Almost every day, I would sit on my bed think of ways to end it all. I couldn't get to mums tablets anymore - she had put a lock on my bedroom door. She was checking my room for stuff nearly every day. I was so low it didn't matter what I did, nothing changed, home life was getting worse still.

"Why"

Every day the rowing became more and more violent between Mum and Alan. A few times I thought he was going to kill Mum. I still didn't like to see Mum get hurt; I tried my hardest to stand up for Mum, although she never stood up for me.

I walked round on eggshells, waiting for him to lash out or just be his evil self.

One morning we was all sitting in the lounge. Alan said, ' I need some money, Sue.'

Mum said, 'Don't look at me, Alan, I am skint until the giro comes in the morning.'

Raising his voice Alan said, 'When that comes I am having all that.'

Mum stood up and shouted, ' No you're not, we need to eat.'

Alan's face red with anger. 'I have fucking told you, I am having that.'

Mum stood right infront of Alan. ' No you're not.'

I was curled up in the corner of the front room, trying to keep out the way.

As I went for the front room door Alan shouted at me: 'You stay where you are.'

With that Alan got to his feet and started laying into Mum. While he was raining punches into her he was shouting 'The money is mine, the money is mine.'

Mum trying to protect her face with her hands as she backed away from him; she was trapped up against the glass coffee table.

With all his weight he pushed her into the glass coffee table, smashing it to bits.

"Why"

Mum was laying amongst the shards of glass in the middle of the floor, with her face all battered and bruised.

Cowering in the corner, seeing Mum's blood covering the floor, I thought that he had killed her and it was now my turn.

Mum started to move on the floor and try to get to her feet.

She groaned, ' Go and get me a tea towel, Marie.'

She wrapped it around her hand; in seconds the tea towel had turned red. She grabbed her coat and left the house.

I was shocked that mum had left me again while he was kicking off.

With Alan pacing up and down the lounge with the glass cracking under his feet. I could tell he was deciding what to do with me. My mind doing overtime - what was he going to do with me now?

"Why"

Chapter Fifteen

He turned to me and said, 'Get your coat your coming with me.' I wanted to tell him to fuck off, but no off I went to got my coat. Wondering where he was taking me, we both left the house. I don't know if it was curiosity or fear, I plunked up the courage to ask, 'Where are we going, Alan? '

He said, 'I am taking you up to see my family, because I think me and your mum are at the end.'

I said, 'The end of what?'

He said, 'I think she has had enough, so I am going to have my fun while I can.'

I said, 'Cant I stay here with Mum?'

He turned and grabbed me by my shoulders and said, 'No you fucking can't - you're mine. '

I knew then I had asked all I could ask.

He let me go and we carried on walking. We got to a long road that lead out of our town.

He put his thumb out cursing as the cars passed us; I was scared out of my wits.

I was thinking in my head why does he think I am his, why wasn't he just going on his own like he normally did? Why was I having to go with him?

After a short walk a car pulled over. The bloke opened his window and asked, 'Can I help? Where are you heading?'

"Why"

Alan said, ' I've got to get up to Cambridge to my mum's because she's not well.'

The man said, 'Jump in. I will be able to take you most of the way.'

Alan ordered me into the back of the car. I sat looking out the window while we drove along. I was nearly wetting myself with fear; he had never taken me before without mum knowing.

I wanted to be back home, but how could I get what I wanted?

He was a lot bigger than me and I was so scared of him. I was like a robot he had the controls of.

The man that was driving had music on and I tried to get lost into it but my fear was far too much.

After a long drive the man pulled over into a lay-by saying, 'This is as far as I can go, mate, I hope your mum's ok.'

He left us at the side of the road. Alan turned and smiled at me. 'Nearly there.'

I just looked at my feet. He put his thumb out again. In the end someone else pulled over and was going where Alan wanted to go. After a short drive this time, the driver pulled over. After Alan said thanks he drove off again.

I was alone with Alan again; the nearer we got to his family the more my mind was racing. We walked down a few streets until we stopped outside a house.

Alan said, 'Come on we are here.'

He knocked on the door; it was Alan's sister that answered it.

"Why"

When she opened the door straight away she said, 'Is the fat bitch with you ?' Alan said, 'No just me and Marie.' she let us in and then she said to me, 'You can sit there and not be seen.'
Pointing to a chair that she wanted me to sit on, I went over and sat looking round the room.
Then for no reason his sister came over and kicked me saying, 'Don't fucking look at me.'
I said, 'I wasn't looking at you.'
I had forgotten myself by answering back. Within seconds Alan was next to me punching me in the face, instructing me, 'Don't even talk to my sister.'
The pain was filling my head; there was blood running down my cheek. They both walked off laughing.
She returned giving me some tissue 'Don't get blood on my carpet.' I took the tissue and said thank you, as she walked off again.
For the rest of the day I had to sit on the chair and not move. When I wanted the toilet I had to put my hand up and ask. Alan would drag me up to the toilet by my hair so I could go. Then drag me right back downstairs again. All day they were drinking beer; I lost count how many. In the evening they got fish and chips. The smell started my stomach rumbling. I got a slapped because they heard the noise my stomach made. They started throwing a few chips at me. Alan said, 'Eat then, you animal.'
I was caught between a rock and a hard place.
Do I leave the chips and get a beating or do I move off the chair and get a beating. I inched forward and leant down picking up the chips.

"Why"

 I probably only had about ten chips at the most in my
hands. Looking at the chips covered in fluff and fag ash
in my hands, I moved my eyes to Alan and his sister;
they were staring at me waiting for me to eat them. I
picked the cleanest chip I could find and popped it into
my mouth. I hadn't been given a drink all day - my throat
was already dry as a bone. Swallowing the fluff covered
chips was making me gag.
Somehow I managed to get the chips down me.
My bottom had no feeling in it and gone numb.
 I tried to rock to get the feeling back but every time I
moved something was thrown in my direction.
They put some music on, turning it up louder and louder
as the empty beer cans piled up on the floor.
I heard a knock at the front door. Alan went to open it
and about ten blokes came in. One of them was his
brother, They all joined in with the drinking.
Then after an hour they all started to get their coats on.
Alan came into the room looking at me with a length of
rope in his hand. He said, 'This is for you just in case
you get any bright ideas.'
His sister grabbed my arms and pulled them behind my
back holding them there while Alan tied them up.
Once he had tied my hands, he kicked my legs against
the legs of the chair.
He wound the rope around my legs lashing them to the
chair legs. He had pulled the rope so tight, I had pins and
needles in my hands and feet. Just before they all left he
said laughing, 'Don't go far, will you.'

"Why"

It was starting to get dark, as I sat there in a strange
house. I looked round the room - there was tin cans
everywhere. The paper from the fish and chips was left
on the coffee table, next to the ash tray that was over
flowing with fag butts; the place smelt really strong of
stale smoke. After a while I wanted to go to the toilet; I
could feel my bladder filling up.

I tried to forget about it but my stomach ached. I must
of held myself for about an hour. It got to much and I
had to go, my bladder emptied where I sat. My trousers
where soaked. It ran off the chair, down my legs and
onto the floor.

I knew I was going to be in really big trouble and I
would get a beating for it when Alan got back. I burst
into tears because I didn't want to make a mess, I didn't
want to be there sitting tied to this chair. I wanted to be
at home or at school with Sally, anywhere but here.

 When they returned, it was only Alan and his sister
with his brother that came back. Someone turned the
light on and Alan saw the wet patch on the floor.

 He staggered over to me, grabbed my hair and pulled
me and the chair over. While I was still tied to the chair
he grabbed my head and rubbed my face into the puddle.
With the urine stinging my carpet-burned face I cried
out, 'I am sorry.'

 But nothing helped. He left me lying on my side, still
with my head in the urine and tied to the chair.

He walked off. I thought that was it, his sister shouted,
'How dare you piss on my floor, you fucking animal.'

"Why"

She came steaming towards me lifting her foot and driving it into my body again and again. She leant down and spat in my face and gave me one more kick and walked away. I was left on the floor for ages until Alan came to right and untie me. Moving my hands and feet to stop the pins and needles.

'Now stand up.' he shouted.

I stood and waited for his next order. 'Come here now.'

I walked into the kitchen where Alan and hie sister were standing next to the back door.

He opened the back door and pointed into the garden. His sister kicking me from behind, shouting, 'Get out there, you animal.'

As I pasted Alan he shoved me out of the door. I tripped and landed on the back doorstep. He followed me into the garden.

'Stand there near that pipe.' he ordered

I got to my feet and moved closer to the wall of the house.

He told me, 'Now Put your arms around the pipe.' With the rope he had used to tie me to the chair, he bound my hands together.

The night air was cold and it had just started to rain. He punched me in the stomach, dropping me to my knees, Saying, 'Oh good its raining, maybe it will wash your pissy trousers, you dirty bitch.'

He went back into the house shutting the door behind him.

The music started as soon as the door was shut. I stood there looking up and down at the iron pipe that ran from the top of the house to the ground.

"Why"

Wondering how long was I going to be out here for and
what was happening to me next.

I know it was raining and cold but I was glad to be
outside, because I was away from the punches and kicks
I got when anyone came near me.

I slid down the pipe and sat on the floor. Looking up at
the rain falling from the sky again asking Nan to come
and get me, but she never came.

After a long time the music stopped; I thought Alan was
going to come and get me, but he never came.

I was left outside all night; the rain didn't let up - it got
harder. My clothes were so wet they were sticking to my
skin.

My whole body was shivering from the cold.

I watched the sky lighten and stood back up, just in case
I got told off for sitting down. I heard someone
unlocking the back door - it was Alan. Leaning on the
door frame he lit a fag and just stared at me. After he
had finished his fag, he undid the rope round my hands.
He took me back inside and up to the bathroom. 'Now
clean yourself up.'

On the floor were a pair of trousers and a top. I washed
myself and got myself dressed; when I came out of the
bathroom Alan was standing there.

Smiling at me, he said, 'That is better - you look nice.'
He took me back downstairs and sat me back on the
chair.

He gave me a bag of crisp 'That is your breakfast - don't
say I don't give you anything.'

I ate the crisp and tried to get myself comfortable,
because I thought I was going to be there all day.

"Why"

I was wrong: after a short while he was giving me my
coat Saying, 'Get ready.'
I thought maybe we was going back home, so I put my
coat on and followed Alan out the door. After a long
walk we both ended up outside another house.
I looked up at the windows; it was run down just like
the house he used to take me to with the horrible men. I
hoped deep down this house was going to be different.
When the door was opened, there was a young lad at the
door, he was only about fifteen. We both went in and the
place was filthy and smelly. Alan said, 'Sit down there.'
pointing at a chair.
 Then Alan went into the kitchen, I could hear him
talking to someone, another man, but I couldn't hear
what they where saying. The young lad sat opposite me,
but he never looked at me - he just stared at his feet.
He had a cut on his face and he was very thin.
Alan came back in telling me. 'Marie, follow me. it's
time to be good.'
We went upstairs and he took me into a bedroom. He
didn't say a word as he left the room closing the door.
The house was silent until I heard footsteps on the
stairs. The door opened and in walked four men. I
gasped and froze. I didn't know what was coming.
The smallest of the men sprayed something into my
eyes. My eyes were stinging and watering, making
everything blurred.
Someone grabbed me and dragged me across the bed,
tying my hands to the bed frame, while another man did
the same with my legs.

"Why"

I could feel the cold steel of a pair of scissors, sliding up my body cutting my clothes off .

Their rough hands wondering all over my naked body then one of them started kissing my body. What ver they sprayed in my eyes was wearing off, my vision becoming clearer.

One of them stood over my head, slapping my face with his penis then forcing it into my mouth. Next to him was a tall man playing with himself.

The smallest man struck a match and lit a fag, sucking on it hard. He came and knelt on the bed, taking the fag from his mouth and touching my stomach with it.

My body jerked as the fag burnt my skin; he then withdrew the fag and licked the burn making me jerk again. He carried on burning me until a fat man pushed him out of the way and climbed on top of me.

The fat man kissed my neck and forced himself inside me.

A hand appeared in front of my face, holding a small canister. Pressing on the top of the canister but nothing came out of the nozzle. I heard someone say, 'Its not working - we will have to do it another way.'

A sweaty piece of cloth was put over my eyes and tied behind my head.

I felt a red hot liquid being dripped on to my body; At the same time I felt warm liquid being poured all over my body and face - It felt like someone was urinating all over me.

They kept climbing on and forcing themselves inside me.

After a while I was untied and sat up on the bed but still blind folded.

"Why"

The bed dipped beside me then the other side dipped.
As a hand held the back of my head and a penis forced
down the back of my throat. He was moving my head
backwards and forwards, making the blindfold come
loose.
He stopped moving my head and removed the blindfold
completely.
A voice from behind me said, 'Bend over the bed.'
I looked down at my body and there was wax all over
my skin and I stank of urine. As I moved I was pushed to
bend over.
I then saw the fat man with this long leather thing, thick
at one end and thin at the other end.
He struck me across my back and bottom - the pain was
unbearable. The small man was bending in front of me
and making me lick his bum.
My poor young body was in so much pain, I thought it
was never going to stop. All of a sudden the door opened
and Alan came in and said, 'OK you have had you time,
now leave her alone. '
I looked at Alan, shocked I thought he was coming to
my rescue.
No, after the men left, another man came in and took his
sick pleasure out on my body.
There was a few more men after him just using my pain
filled body. It stopped. My body battered and sore. I just
wanted to curl up and die. I was given some clothes,
which smelt of smoke and were filthy dirty.
I had nothing else, so I pulled them over my sore aching
body.

"Why"

 I had cuts burns all over my body, the inside of my body feeling like it had been ripped out. Alan took me from the bedroom straight out into the dark street. Once we were walking up the road Alan said, 'I don't have any use for you anymore.' His word sending my mind into overdrive - what did he mean by that? Where was he taking me now? As we approached a park I was convinced he was going to drag me into a bush and kill me.
I wanted to make a run for it, I was feeling weak and in so much pain I knew I wouldn't get far. We crossed the road walking away from the park, I let out a sigh of relief.
I still didn't know what he had planned for me, by the time we arrived back at his sisters house. That night he said, 'Because you have made me lots of money today, you can sleep on the floor and have a blanket.'
When Alan and his sister had left the house, I made my bed on the floor in the corner of the lounge. I pulled the blanket over my head and cried. I just wanted it all to end. I had been asleep for a while, when I heard loads of people in the room with me. I peeked out of the blanket - there was Alan, his brother and sister all drinking. They put some music turning it up full blast.
I put my head back under, hoping they would forget I was there. But no Alan yanked the Blanket off me, I curled up into a ball.
He slurred at me, 'Go upstairs, I will be up soon.'
I got to my feet and went up. I didn't know where he wanted me to go. When I got up there I stood on the landing.

"Why"

Alan came stumbling up the stairs with one hand behind his back. When he reached me he pushed me towards the bedroom. He stank of beer and was slurring his words. He shouted, 'Get on the bed.'
Then he produced a knife from behind his back. With what he said to me on the way back to his sisters running through my mind, I did what he said.
When I was sat on the bed he came towards me and pushed me onto my back.
Falling on top of me, he pushed the knife up at my throat. I just held my breath and stayed as still as I could. He began to touch me and pulling at my clothes until I was naked. He pushed inside me. While he was having his sick pleasure he said, 'You was good today, same again tomorrow.'
I closed my eyes. I couldn't see how my body was going to take anymore punishment.
I wished for him to push the knife into my throat, but no. After he was finished he dragged me back downstairs by my hair. Throwing me back in the corner and spat at me. I grabbed the Blanket and pulled it over me. I watched them all drink more and more.
In time they all passed out. Alan was lying on the floor and his brother was on one of the sofas and his sister on the other.
I sat there quite, thinking about how my body was going to cope with what he had planned for me tomorrow.
A voice inside me kept shouting 'Run.' Over and over again.

"Why"

Run, Marie, get out of here or you will end up dead. I got up slowly and tip-toed towards the front door. When I got there, I looked back and saw that no one had woken up. I turned the handle on the door, it made what seemed like a deafening noise . I looked back at Alan; I froze as he rolled over. I wet myself with the fear that I had just been caught. I stood there for what seemed like a lifetime- luckily he remained asleep.

So I went for it turning the handle and yanking the door open in one move. As soon as it was open, I took off sprinting as fast as my bare feet would take me.

With my legs burning like mad and my lungs bursting I kept going flat out. I didn't have a clue where I was running to but the overwhelming fear of being caught keeping me running.

When I finally run out of steam, I stopped and slumped to the floor, fighting to get my breath back while crying with fear. Once my breathing had calmed down, I had a look round. I was sitting on the pavement; it was dark the street was deserted.

I though to myself, I have made a run for it I have got to keep going. So I picked myself up and started to walk. I kept looking behind me just in case.

Then I saw a pair of car headlights coming up behind me. I jumped over the nearest garden wall, and held my breath.

I thought Alan had woken up and was coming to get me back. When I heard the car pass without stopping, I blew the air out of my lungs.

"Why"

Waiting until I was a bit braver I jumped back over the wall and carried on walking. I didn't know what to do. I thought about knocking on someone's door but I was too scared.

so I just kept walking, not really knowing what to do. Before I knew it there was a car right behind me. I thought about running but I froze to the spot; I dare not look behind me.

I heard the car stop and someone get out. I started to shake with fear, my legs gave way and I ended up on the floor.

I started sobbing saying, 'I am sorry I am sorry.' Over and over again. I covering my head with my hands, waiting for the beating.

I felt a hand on my shoulder. I said, 'Please don't kill me.' A women's voice said, 'it's OK it's OK.'

I turned my head; standing behind me was a policewoman.

That is when I totally lost control. I couldn't speak because I was crying too much. The policewoman bent down to my level saying, 'It's ok, calm down, your safe.' adding, 'Who's going to kill you? What's your name?'

I opened my mouth to speak but again nothing came out. She was joined by another policeman and they helped me to my feet.

They took me to the police car. She opened the door telling me to watch my head and sat me in the back; they both got in. While we drove down the road the women kept trying to speak to me. But still nothing, I couldn't get any words out because I was crying too much.

"Why"

After a while we pulled up outside the police station.
I thought I am in big trouble now as I was taken inside.
They took me to a room which was warm and had a sofa
and a couple of chairs. I was sat on the sofa; the
policewoman made me a hot chocolate. I was then left in
the room alone. I sat there looking round the room; my
mind was racing with worry.

 Then I heard the door open. I jumped out of my skin. In
walked two officers and the policewomen from the car.
One of the police officers placed a tape recorder on the
table in front of me. The policewomen sat next to me,
she took my hand and the man sat in one of the chairs.

 Then the questions started. it was the policeman that
spoke first, I was asked my name, age, where I was
from.

I said, ' Marie Beech, fourteen, Basildon.'

The policeman asked, 'Why do you think you are going
to be killed?'

I then said, 'My mum - please help her, she will be in
danger.'

The policeman said, 'Marie, why do you think your
mum's in danger?'

I said, 'Alan will kill her.'

He said, 'who's Alan? '

I looked down at my feet telling him, 'Alan is the man
who touched me, beat me and he said if I didn't do as I
was told he would kill my mum.'

I begged them to help my mum again. The man pushed
the stop button on the tape recorder and got to his feet.

"Why"

He said to the Policewoman, 'Make Marie something to eat and see if you can find her some clean clothes.'
The policewomen said, 'Yes, OK, I will do that now.'
With that I was left alone again.
 The policewoman came back with a pair of trousers and a jumper.
She asked, 'What do you want to eat Marie?'
I said, 'I don't mind.' food was the last thing on my mind.
She said, 'I will go and find something. I will leave you alone so you can change. '
She then left again. As soon as she walked out the door I got myself changed. The clothes smelt lovely and fresh, not of urine. I sat back down on the sofa and waited, not knowing what was happening. The women returned; she had a steaming hot lasagne, the smell of it making me want it.
I scoffed it down, giving myself hiccups. The policeman returned just as I was finishing my lasagne.
He said, 'We need you to answer some more questions if that is OK?'
I said, 'Is my mum safe? '
He said, 'I have sent some officers to check and I will know soon. '
I said, 'When my mums safe, I will tell you about Alan. '
He said, 'OK Marie, we can wait. '
I wasn't being naughty, but I was worried sick that Alan was going to hurt Mum. I was left alone again. I looked at the window and thought about climbing out and trying to get away. Something kept me sitting though and my eyes started to get heavy - by the time the officers returned I was half asleep.

"Why"

Chapter Sixteen

As soon as someone said, 'Marie, your mum's here. ' I
sat bolt up right as Mum walked into the room with a
policeman.
She looked at me like I was dirt. I looked down at my
feet trying to avoid her eyes. Mum sat next to me and the
policeman started to ask questions again .
Rubbing my shoulders, Mum was playing the caring
mother part in front of the police officers . But I could
tell from the tone her voice that she wasn't happy with
me.
With every word that came out of my mouth, I felt
Mum's eyes burning on me. The policeman that was
asking the questions said, 'Right, we have enough,
Marie, well done, good girl.'
He turned to mum asking, 'Where does Alan's sister
lived?' Mum give him the address.
Mum and the police officers left the room, leaving me
alone with the policewoman. I said, 'Please believe me, I
know I am a child but I am telling the truth, I promise.'
 The policewoman rubbed my knee and said, 'it's ok,
Marie, you have done the right thing.'
 Mum came back in and said, 'Come on, Marie, we have
got to go.'
 I thought we was going home, but no, me and mum
were put in the back of a police car and taken to a small
office block.

"Why"

Two ladies came and greeted us. The officers said, '
These ladies will look after you..' and they drove away.
  Me and Mum were then taken inside, where I was
asked more questions. After what seemed like forever,
the lady told me, 'Marie, you are going to stay with
someone else tonight, like a sleepover. '
I said, 'I want to go home.'
Mum said, 'Marie do what the lady asks.'
I was taken in another police car to a house; a lady
opened the door. She had a soft voice and seemed nice
and friendly. Her home was lovely. I was shown the
bedroom and given some pyjamas. She asked, 'Would
you like a shower?'
 I said, 'No, thank you, I want to go home.'
She replied, 'Maybe tomorrow, but you have to stay here
tonight.'
I asked her 'Where's my mum?'
She told me, 'Mum is back at home.'
 I then freaked out, I ran toward the front door shouting,
'She's in danger. Alan will get her, because I have told
his secret.'
The lady grabbed me and told me, 'Marie, your mum's
ok, the police have Alan.'
I froze. I didn't know what to do. The lady said, 'You
should try and get some sleep.'
She helped me up the stairs and into bed; even though
the bed was warm, clean and comfortable I couldn't
sleep at first.
When I did fall asleep I woke up sweating that Alan was
coming to get me.

"Why"

In the morning the nice lady had made me a lovely breakfast - there was cereal, toast and fresh fruit juice. She gave me some more clean clothes; she insisted that I had a shower first. I took myself to the bathroom and had a warm shower.
When I got back downstairs the lady told me, 'smile - you can go home today, Marie.'
I was happy that I was going home, but scared and anxious at the same time.
Before long two policewomen had come to take me home.
When I got back home, Mum opened the door and hugged me. Mum was being really nice; it was nice being in mums arms.
We all went into the lounge and sat down. The policewomen told mum: 'Alan has been arrested and is being kept on remand.'
Mum just nodded and said, 'OK.'
I didn't know what this meant, but one of the officers said, ' You are safe, he can't come near you.'
The relief was amazing and I could relax for the first time in a long while.
After the police got up and left, I was happy that Mum was being nice to me.
I thought I had the nice mum back, but how wrong was I.
As soon as the policewomen went, mum closed the door and turned to me shouting at me. 'You wait. I am not happy with you. '
I asked, 'Can I go upstairs? ' I thought probably best to keep out her way She agreed.

"Why"

Mum said, 'I will be up soon so don't get comfortable. '
I took myself up and went into my room; it was nice to
be in my safe place again. I heard mum coming up the
stairs, she entered my room with black bags in her hand.
She started throwing all my clothes and stuff into them
and throwing them out the window into the front garden.
I tried to stop her, by grabbing her arm. She wriggled
and got free, slapping me hard round the head and
knocking me to the floor.
She stopped what she was doing and came to where I
had landed.
Standing over me she pounded my body with her feet
while saying, 'You're a dirty slut sleeping with my
husband. I want you out of my house. '
I said, 'I am sorry, but he was bigger than me, Mum, I
couldn't stop him.'
She said, 'No, you're a dirty little tramp.'
She then carried on franticly chucking my stuff out.
When my room was empty she went downstairs. I
remained sitting in the corner wondering why she was
standing up for Alan again.
I then heard mum shout up from outside; I went to the
window. She was pouring some sort liquid on the black
bags holding all my belongings. I ran downstairs, the
best I could after the beating. Limping, I went outside to
speak to Mum. She was lighting a piece of paper with a
match. As soon as the lit paper touched my stuff it all
went up in flames. From her pocket she pulled out a
wade of photographs of me. Throwing them one by one
on to the burning bags shouting,

"Why"

She said, 'You are a dirty whore and your are not welcome in my home. I don't have a daughter called Marie anymore.'

Someone must have gone and got my dad, as I saw him walking towards us. Mum and Dad argued in the street for a while.

Dad was sticking up for me saying, 'Mum was being stupid, you can come with me, Marie.'

He lead me out the gate and walked me away from Mum.

Mum shouting at us, 'Go on, fuck off and don't come back.'

Dad put his arms round me as I started to cry. He took me to his house.

Dad asked, ' Do you want anything, a drink or something to eat?'

I said, 'No I don't fancy anything.'

He said, 'OK I will show you your room. Marie you're going to live with me and Katie now, I hope that's OK?'

I didn't say anything just followed Dad upstairs. I was shown the box room. It had a bed but not much more.

Dad then grabbed my shoulders to get me to face him.

He said, 'Marie you're safe now, you have done nothing wrong. You did the right thing, I just wished you had told me sooner.'

He then let me go and walked toward the door.

Just before he left he said, 'Let me know if you need anything.'

I just looked at my feet and he left. I stood there feeling numb, afraid and confused. My mind was a mess. After a while I lay on the bed and cried myself to sleep.

"Why"

The next week passed in a blur. I couldn't eat because when I did I felt sick. I didn't want to speak to anyone. I stayed in my room most of the time. My dad was a nice man trying his best to help me, but I didn't want anyone's help. I couldn't get my head round why Mum didn't love me anymore. When I had been at Dad's for about a week Dad came into my room. He said, 'Marie I have just been on the phone to the police. There will be a car here in the morning to take you to the hospital.'
I asked, 'Why have I got to go there?'
He said, 'They said they want to check you over to see that you're OK.'
The next morning the police arrived. The policewoman said to me, ' I know you have answered loads of questions before, but would you be able to answer some more questions? but this time it will be recorded on a video camera.'
I asked her, ' Why do I have to answer more questions?' she explained, ' The judge wants to hear what happened.' I stood thinking for a while. I looked at Dad and he nodded.'OK, but when will I have to do it?'
Dad put his hand on my shoulder 'Don't worry, I will be there with you, Marie.'
The policewoman said, ' I will arrange for you to do it as soon as I can.'
I sat in the back of the police car while they took us to the local hospital.
We was taken to a small empty waiting room. A doctor came out of his office and called us in.

"Why"

Dad said, 'I can't do this.'

The policewoman said, 'It's ok, I will come in with you, Marie.'

The doctor examined me and wrote loads of notes, handing them to the policewoman when he had finished. When we arrived home the police said that they would be in touch about the video interview.

A few days later, a police officer came and picked me and Dad up, taking us back to the police station in Cambridge.

I sat in front of a camera, while Dad and the police officer sat behind the camera. After being asked loads of questions by the policewoman, we was taken back home.

Dad took me for lunch at the same cafe that we had gone to on my seventh birthday.

The next week or so passed without much happening.

I asked Dad, ' When can I go back to school?'

Dad said, 'Not for a week or so yet, Marie The court case starts on Monday and you will have to be there.'

I freaked out. ' Will I have to see Alan?'

Dad hugged me. ' No no, it's just in case Alan denies it all; you will be in another room with a policeman.'

I calmed down after Dad's reassuring words, I just hoped he was right.

On the Monday morning of the court case dad woke me up early.

He said, 'You need to try and eat some breakfast, Marie; it's going to be a long day.' I really didn't want anything to eat, but I had some toast just to satisfy Dad.

"Why"

When we arrived at the court in Cambridge a police officer took us into a small room. The room just had a table and a chair and a camera on a stand pointing at me. The officer said, 'Don't worry, it will all be Ok, if we need to ask you anymore questions you won't have to go into the court room.'

I sat on the chair just looking around, Dad left and went into the court room.

The whole morning passed. There was a knock at the door, the police officer opened the door.

Dad walked in and said, 'Alan's a bad man. He is going to prison for twenty years.'

Knowing he was going to be locked up and that I was safe, I put my head in my hands and burst into tears.

Dad held me, saying into my ear, 'He admitted everything, Marie.'

As we left the small room, we bumped into Mum as she was coming out of the court room.

Soon as she see me she started shouting, 'Get that slut away from me, I have lost my husband for twenty years because of her.'

Dad lead me away and took me home. That night I couldn't sleep.

I was still trying to work out why Mum still couldn't see any wrong in Alan.

"Why"

Chapter Seventeen

Two days after the court case, I had to go back to school. My first day back was hard, because I felt that everyone was looking at me and talking about me. When I saw Sally she gave me a big hug. I thought she wasn't going to let me go.

I asked her, ' Do you know what's been going on?' Hugging me again she said, 'Yes my mum told me.' After school that day Sally said, ' I will have my tea and come round to play.' I walked home, worried.

When I got home I told dad, 'Sally is going to knock for me, sorry.'

I was shocked when Dad said, 'Don't be silly, you know you can have friends round and you can play out after school.'

I tried hard to settle in round Dad's. Dad was really nice. He took me to B&Q, letting me choose how I wanted my room decorated.

I picked out some paint, but I don't think I would've cared what colour my room was.

I spent my time at home away from everyone. Katie would say stuff like why did I have to move in, because she had to share Dad. She would push into me when she walked past me; she just couldn't hide the fact she hated me there. I stopped talking to everyone as well, I really struggled with the freedom I now had and how everyone was being so nice.

"Why"

I had been at school for a few days, when the front door bell rang. Dad called me down. There sat in the front room was a lady. She said, 'Hello Marie, I am a social worker, I am here to help you.'

Dad spoke to her saying, ' Marie is back at school but I am finding it hard with clothing her, because her mum has burnt it all.'

The social worker looked shocked but continued on, saying, ' I will sort you out a grant so you can get Marie what she needs.'

She turned to me. ' How are you coping? Is there anything worrying you?'

I kept quite, so she turned back to Dad. He told her, 'I am a bit worried, she has gone into herself.'

She said, ' Marie, would you like to go out with me on my next visit, to a cafe for a drink and a cake?'

I nodded my head and with that she got up and headed for the door.

Before she left she said, 'See you next week, Marie.'

I didn't look up. When she left I went back to my room. I was lying on my bed when Dad came up and said, 'Please talk to me.' I pulled the covers over my head. He then left and went back downstairs.

Later in the week when I got home from school Dad said, 'Marie, don't take your shoes off - we are going shopping.' I put my bag down and stood near the door waiting for Dad. We then both left the house and got into the car and headed towards town.

On the way he said, 'Marie we are going to get you some nice new clothes.'

"Why"

I smiled. Something good was happening to me.
We had been walking round the shops for a while; we
both had loads of bags with all nice new stuff in them.
On the way back to the car, we went into a shoe shop
and got some shoes.
Dad was trying his hardest, but I just couldn't cope.
The social worker visit had came round. Like she said,
we went out for a drink. I started to panic, when she
started to drive towards town.
Speaking for the first time in weeks, I said, 'No we
can't, Alan might see me, I can go there with my dad but
not with you; he hits women.'
She pulled the car over and said in a soft voice, 'Marie
you're safe Alan has been locked up - he can't get you.'
I felt all the weight leave my body, my breathing started
to slow.
I spoke again. 'Are you sure he can't get me, are you
sure?'
She said again, 'Yes Marie, you are safe, so do you want
to go to a cafe?'
I said, 'yes.'I was still anxious
Once we arrived at the cafe, we talked for while
Although I had spoken in the car, I was back to one word
answers.
She told me, 'I am trying to sort out a holiday for you,
Marie, so you can get away and have some fun.'
She asked, 'Do you like living with your Dad?'
I said, 'I can't get use to being able to play out and have
friends round.' I could eat what I liked, watch TV when
I liked. Deep down, I loved it.

"Why"

The social worker sorted out the holiday for me.
On the Friday morning, Dad told me, ' You're not going
to school, you're going away until Monday night.' Fear
ran right through me. When I was with mum normally if
I was having a day off school, I had taken a beating or
something bad was going to happen. I was on edge until
I was picked up. A car pulled up outside my house and
the social worker got out.
She came and knocked on the door; I had already packed
my bag. As we went to walk out the house, Dad handed
me some spending money. I hugged him and said,
'Thank you.'
He said, 'Have fun, Marie, see you when you get back.'
Me and the lady got in the car and drove off down the
road.
I just sat there looking out of the window, it seemed like
we were driving for ages.
Eventually we pulled up at a harbour next to a big ship.
She said, 'Do you like it ?it's like a hotel.'
I said, 'I can't go on there, I can't swim, what if it sinks?'
She said, 'No Marie, it doesn't move; it's stuck in the
mud and the engine doesn't work, so it's OK you will be
fine.'
We both got out and walked towards the ship and up
onto the deck.
A young lady came and said, 'Hi, who do we have here?'
I didn't speak, so my social worker answered, 'This is
Marie and she is staying here for the weekend.' The
young lady was smiling from ear to ear.
My social worker said, 'Can I leave her with you now? I
have got to get back to work.'

"Why"

With that she left me. I was shown a room with loads of
tables, where I was told meals were served. I was then
shown the room I was staying in - it was small with
bunk beds. Another girl was already in there when we
walked in.
Her name was Emily, she was very pretty with long
blonde hair. I noticed she had a nasty scar on her face.
The young lady said, 'Come down at half four for dinner
Emily, will you look after Marie?' Emily nodded and
left us to it.
I couldn't help, but look at her scar. Emily said, 'My dad
did it - he used to hit me and I was taken away and now I
have a new family.'All weekend we stuck together.
When we went down for dinner that evening, there was
loads of kids of all ages. Boys and girls. Me and Emily
sat together. There was one girl that started to call me
and Emily tramps. After a day of her picking on us I had
had enough, I ran towards her and jumped on her back.
With the force she fell to the ground. I started to punch
her in the head. Shouting, 'Stop picking on us.'
The staff pulled me off her. That day I wasn't allowed
off the ship to go crabbing or walk to the park.
Once my curfew had lifted, Emily and me went to the
shop and got some sweets.
The girl still didn't stop picking on us. So when I was
near her room and she was down the park, I went into
her room and nicked her money. I was never found out,
but I think she knew because she left me alone after that.
I put the money back when she stopped bulling us. The
holiday was good, meeting Emily was lovely, but I was
glad to be going home.

"Why"

When I got home, Dad came out and helped me with my bag, asking me loads of question about my holiday. The holiday did cheer me up but I was still struggling with the freedom, I just didn't know what I was allowed to do. I had the freedom of speech as well; I thought my dreams had come true. I Had got the freedom I craved but trouble was I had never had it so, I couldn't deal with it.

"Why"

Chapter Eighteen

So here I was living round Dad's, free, but my head was a mess. Mum didn't want to know me at all. I felt like I had stuck up for her, I kept her safe by taking some of the beatings and all the abuse from Alan. I wish I had shouted at the top of my voice, telling everyone what he was doing to me. I didn't, I was scared, he was a bully. I really thought that if I didn't do as he said mum would be killed.

Now she couldn't even look at me. I was confused and I had this rage building inside me.

Sally started knocking for me nearly everyday. Dad would let her in so that we could listen to music in my room. Sometimes we went out with our friends down to the park. I was still struggling to handle being able to do what I liked

One day when me and my friends were over the park, Four older lads came over to us. They had big brown bottles of booze with them and were smoking joints. Pete, one of the lads, offered me some drink, I thought I looked cool and took a swig. As I gave him back the bottle he offered me his joint.

I took it and had a drag and offered it back to him. It tasted and smelt different to the normal fags I smoked. After a few drags on it, I felt light headed and numb. I started to laugh at nothing, I felt good and the bad thoughts in my head started to fade away.

"Why"

After that evening I meet up with these older lads more often. Sally came sometimes but she didn't like them so much.

I liked the drink and drugs they always had.

I was staying out for the night sleeping on the bedroom floor at Pete's house. Dad started to tell me off, because I was drunk most of the time. I became rude telling Dad he couldn't tell me what to do, because he hadn't cared all them years before, he didn't have a right to try to be my Dad now.

I just couldn't get enough of the drink and drugs. It blocked out all the thoughts that were going round in my head. School wasn't much better, I started getting into fights all the time.

A girl that knew what had happened to me called me a skank. I lost it and beat her up, stamping on her head. People had to pull me off of her, I am glad they did. Looking back now I would've probably caused some real damage to her.

My learning at school went out of the window. I just didn't care about anything. I started to steal from shops, to pay for my drink and drugs.

Sally told me that she missed her friend - deep down I missed her too. But she didn't like the friends I was hanging out with.

I used to meet up with Sally, but as soon as we bumped into my new friends I would go off with them. I knew I could block out my memory with them, or with what they had. A girl called Claire started to hang round with me. She went to the same school as me, she was picked on all the time.

"Why"

 I would stick up for her - she had the gob but couldn't
back it up. She liked to drink as well, and she became a
close friend. School often contacted Dad, telling him I
had done something I shouldn't have. Every telling off
he gave me, made me fight back.

 It would make me stay out more nights. Pete and the
lads used to go round to a flat. Everyone there would be
drinking and smoking.

Nearly every day I would take the stuff I had stolen over
there and sell it. I wouldn't sell it for money, I would sell
it for more drink and drugs. I wouldn't be in control of
my actions, I was too pissed. Every now and then, I
would be walking down the road with my friends or on
my own. I would bump into mum and she would start
shouting abuse at me. One day I was pissed out of my
mind when I bumped into Mum. Again she started
shouting. I don't know if it was the drink that gave me
the courage, but I let her have it. I told her, 'Alan was
going to kill you, if I didn't do what he wanted, so I let
him to keep her safe.'

She said, 'You're lying, You just wanted my husband for
yourself.' I shouted at her ,'You make me sick, I wish I
had said no and fought him and not taking anything to
keep you safe.'

With that she walked off. My new friends knew nothing
of my past, So after mum had walked off, they asked,
'What was that all about? Why does your mum hate
you?'

I said, 'She is a stupid women with mental problems.'
And left it at that. I didn't want my friends to know the
truth about my past.

"Why"

When I was at home alone in my room, my thoughts
would drive me crazy. I would rock on my bed crying
until I fell asleep. I think I was just a frightened young
girl trying to make some sense of her life.

On one of my social work visits she said, ' I have
arranged for you to talk to someone. It might help,
because your dad is worried about you.'

I replied, 'I don't want to talk to anyone.'

A few days after her visit I was in a car being taken to
see someone.

I kept quite most of the way and just sat looking out of
the window, until I saw a sign for Cambridge which was
Alan's home town. I freaked out. I thought they were
taking me back to him. The car was still moving when I
went for the door handle Shouting, 'Why are you taking
me to Alan's? He will kill me.'

I carried on pulling at the door handle but the door
wouldn't open. The women pulled over and got out and
came round to my door. As soon as the door was open, I
tried to do a runner. She grabbed my arm and said,
'Marie, you are safe, Alan is in prison.'

I said, 'What about his family? Maybe they will kill me
for him. I am not going anywhere. I just want you to
take me home.'

She said, 'Calm down, Marie, let's just go and see the
doctor, then as soon as you are finished I will take you
straight home. I won't leave you on your own.'

She closed the door and got back into the car and carried
on driving. I was trying hard not to wet myself with fear,
as we got nearer to Cambridge.

209

"Why"

Eventually we pulled up outside an old building. As we left the safety of the car my heart was pounding. My eyes were scanning everywhere trying to spot Alan's family. Once we was inside the waiting room, I sat facing the door checking everyone that came in and out. A women came out of a room; she called out my name, asking me into her office. I went in and took a seat; she started to ask me loads of questions.

She had a way about her, too nice, she was well dressed, her hair put up in a nice bun. I thought to myself she knows nothing so I asked her, ' Do you have a nice mum and dad ?'

she answered, ' I have a lovely family, I grew up on a farm.'

That was it: I shouted, 'So what do you know about how I am feeling? You know nothing. How dare you sit there coming from a lovely home, great job, lovely clothes and ask me how I am. Well I am telling you nothing, I am going now - you make me sick.'

I stormed out and said to the lady that had brought me, 'Take me home now and I am not coming back.'

On the long drive home I said nothing the rage inside me was boiling. When I got home, I ran up to my room and started to smash it up. I just couldn't stop. I hit the door and felt a pain shoot up my arm. I dropped to my knees holding my hand and crying uncontrollably.

Dad knocked on my door. I opened my mouth but couldn't answer him. He came in, seeing me on the floor. He wrapped his arms round me; it felt so good.

He noticed my hand. 'I think we need to get that hand looked at.'

"Why"

I said, 'Sorry about my room.'
He said, 'Don't worry about it, let's just get you to
hospital, Marie.' Dad helped me downstairs and told
Katie, ' I am taking Marie to the hospital.'
 She said, 'OK dad. is Marie ok?'
He said, 'I think she has broken her hand.'
When we got to the hospital, the doctor pulled my hand
about saying to dad, 'I think we better x-ray her hand.'
 Dad said, 'Do you think its broken?'
The doctor said, 'I think it might be; wait out in the
waiting room and someone will call for you for the x-
ray.'
We both walked back out to the waiting room. It was
packed with loads of different people. Some with cuts
and bruises, some with hands like mine, and people who
looked like death warmed up.
We took a seat next to a lady that had her shoe off; her
toes were black. She smiled at me. 'Looks like you have
been in the wars just like me.'
Dad said, 'Yes, she fell over, bless her.'
I looked at dad, wondering why he hadn't told the truth
about me being naughty and stupid and smashing my
room up.
Dad held my good hand and said, 'Are you ok, Marie, do
you want a drink?'
I answered, 'Yes please, if I'm allowed.'
Dad got up and walked over to the machines; he came
back with a can of coke and a coffee for himself. We
sat there for ages, until a nurse came out and called my
name. I followed her into the x-ray room.

"Why"

 I had to keep it really still; Dad had to wait outside.
While the machine was working the lady stood behind
this big glass wall. She said, 'Right, all done; if you take
a seat back out in the waiting room the doctor will call
for you soon.'
So yet again we was sitting waiting. I was starting to get
bored.
Me and Dad was called again. We went into the room
with the doctor.
He said to dad, 'She's got a chip out of her bone, so we
won't put it in plaster. we will give you pain killers. she
will have to be careful for a few days.'
A nurse put a sling on me and we was allowed to go.
We walked to the car and got in. Before Dad started the
car dad turned in his seat and asked, 'Marie why did you
smash up your room?'
I thought I was in trouble, thinking Dad was going to
beat me, so I said nothing. Dad leaned over to give me a
hug. I flinched because I thought he was going to hit me.
He saw that I was cowering away.
He said, 'Marie, I will never hit you, you're safe with me.
Oh darling, I am so sorry if I frightened you - I was only
going to hug you. '
I looked at dad and started to cry. I said, 'I am sorry I
smashed up my room.' Dad said, 'But why, Marie? I can't
help you if you won't talk to me, sweetheart.' Again I
said nothing.
Dad turned back in his seat and started the car.
When we arrived home, I went up to my room and
started to clean up the mess I had made.

"Why"

Dad called me down and asked, 'Marie, do you want fish and chips tonight?' I answered, 'Yes please if I am allowed. '

Dad said, 'Of course your allowed, Marie, what do you want?'

I said, 'Chips please.'

Dad replied, 'Do you not want anything with them? Maybe a sausage, fish cake, pie ? ' 'Can I have a sausage with my chips please?'

I couldn't believe I could have more than just chips.

Dad got his coat and shouted as he went out the door: 'Won't be long girls.'

Katie was sitting on the sofa watching TV. When dad left Katie looked at me. 'Why did you have to come here? you're just trouble. '

I said, 'No I am not, Katie, shut up.'

She kept on. 'No I wont. I hate you being here, Marie.'

I ran towards her grabbing her hair, and started to hit her. We ended up rolling around the floor hitting each other. We didn't notice Dad come back. He pulled us off each other. Making us sit on the sofa, he said, 'What the hell is going on here? Marie, you're supposed to be keeping your hand safe. Hitting each other is wrong; I won't have it. Why was you fighting?'

Both of us sat in silence. Dad walked off and took the dinner into the kitchen.

Me and Katie remained sitting on the sofa. Dad then called us to get our tea. When I walked in I was shocked I had loads of chips and two sausages. We all sat round the dining table and tucked in. We were nearly finished eating.

"Why"

Dad said to both of us: 'Right girls, we all have to live together so I wont have anymore fighting - you're sisters, you're supposed to look after each other. '
We both said, 'OK dad sorry. '
After dinner dad cleaned up; it was bed time for me and Katie. I was getting into bed, Dad came in and kissed me goodnight. He knelt down near my bed and said, 'Marie, if you need me or want to talk to me you know where I am.'
He then kissed me again, got to his feet and left the room. I lay looking up at the celling trying to sort out my messed-up head.
When I was walking to school the next day. I intended on go in. I was going to try hard for Dad to sort myself out and behave.
I sat in the classroom and all the bad feelings and thoughts were racing through my head. So when it came to lunch time I was ready to run.
I headed across the field, jumped over the fence and started to walk to the park. When I arrived some of my mates were there.
I walked over and said hi to them; as soon as I reach them I was handed a can of beer. They asked what I had done to my hand, I didn't tell them - I just fobbed them off.
I spent all afternoon with them, only going home to get changed. By this time I was half pissed. I opened the front door and ran the best I could up to my room. I didn't speak to Dad; I knew he would smell the booze. I got myself changed. On my way down the stairs I shouted out to dad.' I am going out.'

"Why"

He shouted back, ' Be home for nine.'

'OK.' I yelled as I closed the door.

I went back to the park to meet my friends. That night I drunk so much, I had trouble walking home, so two of my friends took me home.

 When they knocked on the door Dad opened it up. He saw the state of me and helped me in.

He helped me up the stairs and gave me a bowl as I was saying that I was feeling sick. Dad stayed with me. Holding my hair out of the way, he stayed until I was asleep.

In the morning my head was banging. Dad went mad when I went downstairs, saying that I was stupid drinking so much that people had to bring me home.

 He said that I had to talk to someone if not to him, he said I needed help.

I just grabbed some toast and left for school, not that I went. None of my friends were at the park when I got there.

So I went round and knocked for them; when I got there they said that they where going to the beach. One of the boy's older brother drove. I was asked along. We all squeezed in to his gold mini - with Claire and me there was seven of us. We had to sit on the boy's laps and we all set off.

We all started to smoke. I am surprised the driver could see through the smoke. The buzz I got from the drugs started making me forget everything. When we got to the beach we walked round the arcades. We didn't go on the rides because none of us had enough money on us.

"Why"

Me and Claire only had our dinner money. I was lucky
on one of the machines: I put fifty pence in and won six
pound. I had some candy floss and got me and Claire a
bag of chips for lunch. I gave the driver two pound
towards the petrol - everyone did expect Claire as she
had used all hers. I really enjoyed the day; we didn't get
home until it was dark. Dad didn't tell me off as he
thought id been to school and then went out with my
friends after.
 I felt bad about lying to Dad, but I couldn't get enough
of the drink and drugs. It helped with my head, but at
night the nightmares scared me and kept me awake.
Most of the time I would close my eyes and see Alan
standing over me, holding me down with a knife saying,
'I told you not to tell.
 I would wake me up sweating, then I was to scared to
try again to sleep.
Dad did his best to help me, but I didn't want help from
anyone; I just wanted to forget.

"Why"

Charter Nineteen

My relationship with my sister wasn't getting any better.
When ever we past each other, we would punch or kick
one another. She didn't like me being there. I hated her
for going to live with Dad and having a good life, while
I was stuck at home with mum and that monster.
The social worker came round once a week, taking me
out, when I could be bothered to be there.
One afternoon when I got home, Dad told me off for not
being there to see the social worker. When he had
finished telling me off, he took me upstairs to show me
my new bed that the social worker had got me.
Often Dad would come up in my room, when I was
having time to myself. He would try his hardest to talk
to me, but I still hated myself, I still felt dirty and I
didn't want Dad or anyone to judge me.
I loved my dad with all my heart, I didn't want Alan's
memories anywhere near Dad.
I was still not going to school, skipping it to be with my
friends. Claire was seeing one of the lads we hung
around with.
Pete one of the other lads, started making noises that he
liked me and asked a few times to be my boyfriend. I
turned him down flat; I wasn't interested.
One night we was at the flat where I sold my stolen
stuff. The flat was owed by an old bloke that liked his
drink; he lets us just come and go when we pleased.

"Why"

 On this night we was drinking and just hanging out, I
had not had much to drink. Me and Claire and a few
other girls that was there was lying on the bed. I
must've dosed off - when I woke up all the other girls
had gone and Pete was on top of me.
He had me pinned down, I couldn't move. His hands
wondering, touching me just like Alan did. He tried to
undo my trousers; I exploded. I started to hit him, he
slapped me round the face. I'd harder from Alan. I
kicked my legs to try and get him off me.
He whispered in my ear, 'Come on, Marie, you know
you want me. '
Still kicking and hitting out, I shouted, 'Get off me,
please let me go. '
I burst into tears, but he still wouldn't get off me.
He said, 'You're a tease, Marie, you have been giving me
the come-on for weeks now; open your legs. '
One of my flailing kicks caught him where it hurts. He
rolled off me holding himself, I got up as fast as I could.
Before I could get to the door, he was grabbed me and
pushed me up against the door.
He was on me again, I was wondering why wasn't
anyone helping me.
He started to kiss me, pushing his face into mine. I was
fighting to get free; as he moved his face away I spat at
him. He came back again, trying to kiss me, I sank my
teeth into his lip as hard as I could.
He backed off holding his lip and looking at his hand
covered in blood. I managed to get the door open and
ran into the front room. It was empty; I was alone.

"Why"

I ran to the front door looking over my shoulder. As soon as it was open, I ran for it. I kept going until I ran out of breath. When I stopped running, I was far away from the flat.

I went to the park and sat on the swing crying. I sat there for a while, trying to work out why people just wanted to use me all the time. It started to get cold. I pulled myself together and I took myself off home, thinking about what had happened all the way.

I wasn't going to tell, because I thought I had done something wrong. As soon as I got home, Dad must've sensed something.

He walked over to me and as soon as he said, 'Marie are you ok?'

I lost control - all my feelings came out at once. 'Dad I must be a bad person because people want to hurt me. ' I repeated it a couple of times.

Dad said, 'Marie has something happened?' I said, 'I am sorry, dad, I am dirty.' Dad said, 'Marie, you're not dirty, your my princess.'

After a lot of coaxing, Dad got out of me what had happened. He called the police; they came round and asked me questions. That night was a massive turning point in my life. I realised I had someone who loved me and cared about me.

A few of my mates that I hung around with took Pete's side.

But some of them took my side. Claire came round a couple of days after the attack and hugged me, Saying, 'Oh Marie, I am so sorry for leaving you.'

"Why"

I said to her, 'Don't worry, you wasn't to know that was going to happen.'
She hugged me again and we went up to my room and listen to some music. Pete was arrested and got three months in prison for attempted rape.
 Weeks after that Dad helped me; he kept talking to me all the time. It wasn't to last - not because of anything Dad did -It was just my pasted showing its ugly head again. It was nice to have Claire by my side but I did miss my friend Sally. I felt horrid how I had dropped her for my new friends. The next day I plucked up the courage and went round to Sally's house. She let me in straight away; we talked about how we had missed each other.
I said, ' I would like us to see more of each other.'
Sally said, 'I like Claire, but I don't like most of your other friends that you hang out with - that's why I stopped knocking for you.'
After that day it was me, sally and Claire hanging out. When I was alone, I was still drinking; I tried to stop drinking but I couldn't handle the stuff that was going round in my head all the time.
I was fourteen now - my fifteenth birthday was coming up.
I didn't give birthday much thought; It had never been a special day.
When dad walked in to my room with a card and a present I actually asked him, 'What is this for?'
Dad laughed, 'It's for your birthday.'
I had totally forgotten. I sat up in bed and took the present dad handed me.

"Why"

I ripped the paper off; it was a new school bag and a voucher for some clothes. I hugged Dad and said, 'Thank you.'

He said, 'Marie, I'd loved to give you a party, but I cant afford one I am really sorry - maybe next year.'

I said, 'Don't worry, Dad its ok.'

When Dad left, I got myself up and got dressed for school. When id had my breakfast, I asked 'Dad can I go round Sally's after school?'

He agreed. I hugged and kissed Dad and left the house. I knocked for Sally on the way, Claire meeting us half way to school.

That day dragged. I didn't tell Sally it was my birthday till after school. When we got to her house, she told her mum and she gave me some money.

Sally said, 'Right you're going on the calendar so I don't forget again.' I laughed at her. Sally's mum was so nice, we had pizza for tea. While we was eating she went to the shop, getting us loads of sweets and crisp for us girls to share. She said, 'Sorry for forgetting.'

How could I be mad - I had forgot my own birthday! It was nice to be hanging out with Sally again. When I was walking home that night, a blue car passed me really slowly then sped off, only to drive passed again and again. I was getting worried something didn't feel right, so I ran home.

I saw the car the next day going to school, then a couple of more times after school; it always slowed down but never stopped. I was coming back from Sally's house one evening; again there it was but this time the car pulled up beside me.

"Why"

The door flew open and I was grabbed by a man.
He dragged me into the car. When I looked round the car
I shit myself. Sitting in the front seat, looking straight
back at me, was Alan's sister.
Another was a man driving and a man sitting beside me.
I nearly wet myself with fear. I thought they had come to
kill me for Alan.
We drove for awhile out to the countryside; the driver
turned down a dark lane. I really thought this is it. The
car came to a stop. I was ordered out of the car; the two
men didn't move. It was only Alan's sister that got out
with me.
I stood there wondering what was going on. She came
closer punching and kicking me.
I fell to the ground. She stamped on my head, my eyes
puffing up, closing gradually, blood running from my
nose and mouth. She didn't leave any part of my body
alone, beating me black and blue.
She stopped taking a handful of my hair she lifted my
head off the ground, turning my head in her direction. I
could just about make her face out through my closing
eyes. 'This is for Alan, you dirty scum, and if you tell
anyone who did this to you, we will be back.'
Dragging me to my feet by my hair,she pushed me
towards the car again.
I couldn't hardly walk; my legs and body was in so much
pain. After a short drive, the car pulled over again. The
door was opened again.
I was told, 'Get the fuck out of my car and remember
don't tell because next time we will kill you.'

"Why"

The man sitting next to me lifted his leg and kicked me
out of the car.
I landed on the pavement as the car drove off at speed.
Pulling myself up I sat on the pavement hurting all over.
I sat there for a while, then managed to get to my feet.
I had been dropped off where they had picked me up. I
staggered home the best I could holding on to garden
fences and wall to hold me up.
When I knocked on the door dad opened up. I thought
he was going to tell me off for being late home. When
he saw me, I could see the shock and worry on his face.
He helped me in and sat me on the sofa. He was just
about to ring the police. When I shouted, 'Please, Dad,
don't.'
He said, 'Marie, we have to tell them. '
' I am begging you, Dad, please don't call the police.'
He said, 'OK but you have to tell me who did this to
you.'
I said, 'I can't - they will kill me. Please don't tell the
police.'
He said, 'OK Marie, but please talk to me.'
I said, 'No I can't, please leave it, Dad.'
With that he got up and went into the kitchen, coming
back with some cotton wool and warm water. He started
to clean me up. One of my eyes was completely closed
and the other one was just about open with the swelling .
After Dad had patched me up he helped me up to bed.
He lay me on the bed and pulled the covers over me.
He said, 'Marie, I wish you would tell me who did this to
you - it's wrong.' Again I begged him to leave it.
He then left me to get some sleep, it never came that
night.

"Why"

The slightest noise made me jump out of my skin. The
pain my body was in didn't help either.
In the morning, Dad came into my room. He said, 'Your
not going to school today, you're not well enough. Have
you change your mind about telling me who did this?'
I just said, 'Please Dad, don't, I can't tell you I am sorry.'
I went downstairs. Katie was shocked when she came
down to go to school.
She asked, ' What happened to you, Marie?'
I told her, 'Some kids jumped me last night.'
She was happy with my answer she said, 'What was you
gobbing off?'
I didn't answer, Dad came into the kitchen and said,
'Marie, I have got to go to work, but I don't want you
going out, please don't go out.'
I said, 'I wont, Dad, I am staying in.'
He smiled at me and finished getting ready for work.
Just before he left for work he kissed me on the head and
said again, 'Please don't go out, I will worry about you.'
He then left.
I was lying on the sofa watching video's in an empty
house. I got as comfortable as I could and drifted off to
sleep. I was woken up by a loud knock at the door.
I pulled the covers over my head and stayed there.
I didn't move until I felt safe again.
I got up to go to the toilet, my body aching; my eye was
completely closed now.
I had bruises all over my body. Every time I moved the
pain would remind me of Alan's sister's words.

"Why"

I lay there on the sofa speaking to Nan, asking her why people hated me so much and I asked why she left me behind. I felt so alone, even though Dad was everything I had wished for.

He was a lovely man but Alan's evil was still haunting me. He was still controlling me, I couldn't eat; inside I was a scared girl.

The only thing that helped me was drink. So that just what I turned to. It was around lunch time - I knew I had a few beers in my room. So I struggled up the stairs to fetch them. I sat on my bed and drank them straight down, but they weren"t enough.

I didn't go out that day because I had promised Dad but the following day, I took the ten pound note that Sally's mum had given me for my birthday.

After everyone else had left the house I got dressed and went out, going straight to the flat where Pete tried to rape me. I didn't care I just needed to get drink and drugs.

When I got there the old boy was pleased to see me; he was really sorry that he wasn't at the flat to help me that day. I stayed there all day and got totally out of my head on drink and drugs. When it was time to go home, I could barely walk. I got home and Dad was angry, but I didn't care.

I didn't care about anything anymore, I thought if I was a bad person then I had to be bad. I went back to my bad ways. Dad begged me to stop but I didn't listen.

I felt like I was cracking up; I didn't want to be alive anymore. I didn't care what happened to me anymore. I hated myself and thought everyone else hated me.

"Why"

Walking back home one evening, I turned the corner and in front of me stood mum. She started to shout abuse at me. I walked right up to her. My nose was nearly touching hers. I told her, 'Go and fuck yourself, you're a crap mum, I am not the one who let you down - it was the other way round.'

She pushed me away and I saw red. I slapped her round the face. I said, 'I have no mum anymore.'

I think it was the drink that gave me the balls - even though she wasn't as strict as Alan she give me a few beatings.

I had never stood up to her before. I hated her because I kept her safe. Well that's what I thought because Alan said do as I say and I won't kill your mum. I was mad: I had saved a women who didn't care about me.

I walked off , she shouted, 'Go on! I 've got no daughter anymore either.' A tear rolled down my cheek. I wiped it away.

I wasn't going to cry and be weak. I kept drinking every day. I stopped going to school again.

Dad kept saying, 'Marie you have your exams coming up.'

I couldn't give a toss about the exams. All I was worried about was my next drink or joint - preferably both.

"Why"

Chapter Twenty

I was lost to drink and drugs and I had pushed dad to the limit. Arriving home from another one of my days of drinking, I was lying on my bed trying not to be sick, when dad walked in. He wasn't alone: my social worker was with him. I had not seen her in ages.
I had been out every time she had come round to the house.
I told them to leave. Dad raised his voice for the first time since I had moved in with him. He said, 'No, Marie, I won't watch you destroy your life.'
My social worker sat on my bed trying to talk to me.
I snapped at her, 'Get off my bed.'
Dad shouted, 'Marie, don't be rude - she is here to help you.'
I said, 'I don't want anyone's help; I am not worth helping.'
She got up and left the room.
Dad sat on the bed lowering his voice. He said, 'Marie, I love you, please talk to someone. '
I lifted my heavy head off the pillow and looked up at Dad's face. He looked so sad and deflated. He left my room, as I curled up in to a ball trying not to be sick.
I lay there and all I could think of was Dad's face. I wanted to hurt myself but not my dad. I hauled myself off the bed and went downstairs.
Sitting in the front room was dad and the social worker.

"Why"

I went over to dad and said, 'Help me then please, I can't take it anymore; help me forget, stop the nightmares I have every night.'

He stood up and took me in his arms, hugging me. He said, 'Marie, I will do my best, sweetheart.'

After that day, I was sent to a lady at a health centre and asked loads of questions. I was economical with the truth. I didn't tell the lady that I thought I was bad, dirty and not worth saving and that I thought about ending it nearly everyday.

I was prescribed some tablets. Dad had to keep them, giving me one tablet every night. The tablets helped me fall asleep, but again id be asleep for a few hours only to wake in a cold sweat.

Sometimes I would be screaming, Dad would rush in and hold me.

He said, I would be sat bolt upright in bed, My eyes open but not awake. He would lie me back down again.

It got so bad at night the doctors talked about giving me an injection at night, I wasn't up for that.

I don't know if it was talking to the lady at the health centre or the medication working - but it started to get a little easier to sleep at night.

I was just a lost teenage girl trying to find her way back to normal, safe life. I never told who beat me up that night, their warning was to freighting. Because I had messed up my school leaving with nothing, Dad got me into a course at college.

"Why"

Helping me with reading and my maths, the good thing was Sally and Claire went to the same college. So I saw them everyday which helped me, I tried my hardest at college and made more friends.

Every now and then one of Pete's friends, who knew what had happened to me in the flat, would say something. When I couldn't handle it, I would leave college and go and sit in the park, wishing the ground would open up and swallow me whole.

Life felt like it was getting easier, but I was still temped to have a drink now and again. I liked the numb feeling it gave me.

I think Dad was happy that I was behaving better; I must have been hard work for him. He was trying to be there for us girls, hold a job down and keep the house running. Dad never really went out much; he would go down the pub for an hour but he was always home before us, with our tea ready. Katie had got herself a boyfriend, so he was round for tea some nights.

He was nice but me and Katie was still horrid to each other most of the time. Katie went to college as well, doing a computer course. She would call me a thicko because of the courses I was doing at college and we would end up fighting.

Dad was more like a referee than a dad, when it came to me and Katie.

I tried to stay up in my room out of Katie's way Most evenings. Sally and Claire would come round and hang out. By this time Dad knew I smoked. He wasn't happy about it but I think he didn't have the fight in him to stop me; I was just told to never smoke in my room.

229

"Why"

One day Dad wasn't at home when I got in. I soon found
out he wasn't far away - he was next door. Some people
had just moved in that day, and Dad was helping them.
Moving in was a women her two older children, a boy
and a girl and a girl a year younger than me.
Dad must of seen me in the garden having a fag.
 He called over the fence, 'Marie is that you?'
I replied, 'Yes, dad, its me, what you doing over there?'
Dad said, 'Helping. I will be back in a minute.'
'Ok see you soon,' I replied; with that he was gone back
inside.
I finished my fag and went back indoors. After a little
while I heard the front door go and Dad saying, 'Marie, I
am home sweetheart.'
I came down to see Dad. He was in the kitchen and
starting to cook dinner.
 I sat on one of the dining chairs, asking questions about
the people that had moved in next door.
Dad said, 'You can asks them yourself - they are coming
for tea, as their cooker isn't set up yet. It will only be
Jenny and Gill as her older children would still be at
work.' I left dad too it.
After being in my room for a bit with Dad's cooking
smells wafting up the stairs, I heard the door go and then
Dad calling me down. I turned my TV off and went
down. Sitting at the table was a girl and a lady. I said,
'Hi.' and sat down.
I asked, 'Where's Katie?'
Dad said, 'She's staying round her boyfriend's tonight.'
I turned to talk to our new neighbours. Jenny said she
was going to be starting at the same college as me and
Katie.

230

"Why"

Dad suggested that I could walk with Jenny in the morning and look out for her. I wasn't sure about it, but agreed because Dad had asked me. After dinner me and jenny went up to my room; Dad and Gill shared a bottle of wine downstairs. We listened to some music and chatted, Jenny wasn't bad.

She told me that she had only just lost her dad seven months ago and she was really missing him. I felt for her thinking to myself how sad and alone I would be if I lost my dad.

It was time for them to go home, as it was getting late. When they had left dad came up to my room and said, 'Thanks, Marie, for having jenny in your room - she hasn't got any friends down here. '

I said, 'That's Ok, Dad, she seemed nice. '

Dad said, 'Anyway it was nice of you, I know you don't like people in your room.'

I teased Dad saying, 'So, Dad, Gill going to be coming round a lot? '

Dad laugh and said, 'Marie, behave.' He left me to settle down for the night.

In the morning I knocked for jenny and we walked to college. When we got there I took jenny to the office and said, 'Meet me here at the end of the day and we can walk home together.'   I left to go and find my friends.

When I found Sally and Clare they asked where id been. I told them about jenny and told them she would be walking home with us. From then on Gill and jenny was always round. It became obvious that jenny had her mum wrapped around her little finger. Jenny would say jump and her mum said how high?

231

"Why"

Gill was always telling me what to do, like pick up your stuff, don't smoke too much - it started to get on my nerves because she was nothing to do with me. Jenny started to hang out with me and my friends - not that I asked her along. I just felt like I had to take her along. Some days I couldn't get out quick enough to avoid Jenny.

She did come in handy sometimes though; she always had money on her. So she brought the fags or other stuff.

One day I came home to Dad and Gill sitting on the sofa. As soon as I walked in Gill started shouting at me saying I was a thief.

I shouted back, 'I haven't stolen anything, now fuck off out of our house.'

Dad stood up and came over and put his hands on my shoulders and told me to 'calm down.'

I stopped shouting. I thought he believed me, but no, Dad asks me again.

I pushed dad off me and stormed out the house; I was steaming. I know I had stolen from shops but never from friends. I was so mad that dad had taken Gill's side, I stayed round Sally's that night.

Still filled with anger the following morning we left for college. All day the though of being accused of being a thief was going around my head.

When I got home I headed straight to my room. Dad came up to speak to me. I wasn't interested in what he had to say, so he gave up and left me alone.

Jenny came round. 'Are you coming out, Marie?'

I said, 'I am not in the mood but you can come up and hang out if you want .'

"Why"

She came up into my room. We put some music on and chatted. When Jenny went to the bathroom the music stopped so I got up to change the tape over. As I was getting up, Jenny's bag fell off the bed. I picked up all her stuff that had fallen out, and noticed she had loads of money in her purse. I just thought at that moment lucky girl; I put everything back and carried on with what I was doing.

When Jenny got back I asked, 'Have you any fags?'
She said, 'No, I don't have any pocket money either.'
I said nothing but thought it was weird. I went down and nicked a fag off dad. Gill was downstairs and looked at me like I was dirt. I took no notice and went into the garden for a smoke.

A couple of weeks passed, then Dad broke the news to me and Katie that him and Gill was together, I hated the idea. Over the next few months Gill was at our house more and more; in the end never went home. Eventually it became permanent. Gill and Jenny moved in just before Christmas leaving her older children to look after her house.

One evening I was told to sit down in the lounge with Dad and Gill sitting opposite me. Dad leaned forward in his chair ' Marie, have you taken some Christmas club vouchers out of Gill's bag?'
I said, 'What vouchers?, I don't know what your on about.'
Gill piped up, ' Come on, Marie, think hard; you must know what we are talking about.'
I stood up shouting, 'Fuck off, I am not a thief.' And stormed out.

"Why"

The vouchers were not mentioned again but there was an
atmosphere in the house. If I was about, Gill would keep
her bag with her. Just a few days before Christmas Day
me and Jenny was hanging out in my room. We was
talking about going out, so Jenny went into her purse to
check how much money she had. As she was checking,
her mum called her down; she left her open purse on
my bed. I saw a voucher poking out of her purse. I
stormed downstairs and ordered Dad outside. Telling
him what I had seen.
He went back in and said to Gill, 'It wasn't Marie that
had taken the vouchers out of your bag, it was Jenny.'
Straight away she said, ' You're making it up, Barry,just
to get Marie off the hook and out of trouble.'
Dad said, 'I think it would be best if you leave, Gill.'
she was never going to believe that her sweet little girl
would thieve from her. So they both moved back next
door. Christmas came and went. Just before new year's
eve I came home from being out with my friends.
I found Gill in our front room with Dad. We both
looked at each other but didn't say a word to each other.
Dad said, 'Gill wants to forget all that stuff that
happened before Christmas.'
I nodded and left the room and took myself to my
bedroom. While I was sitting in my room there was a
knock at my bedroom door.
 I said, 'Come in.' expecting it to be Katie or Dad.
The door opened in walked Jenny. she said, 'Could we
talk?'
I said, 'ok.' she came in and sat on my bed.

"Why"

She said, ' I didn't take the vouchers, Mum gave me a couple.' I couldn't prove it, so we left it at that.
Jenny was a nice girl and we did get on - life was back to normal.

Gill and Jenny moved in again, Every now and then id over hear Gill talking to Dad about me taking money from her bag. I didn't say anything; I knew I hadn't taken anything. Dad seemed happy with Gill. I didn't want him to lose the happiness, so I thought let her hate me.

Me and Jenny were hanging out in my room and getting ready to go out.
Jenny was having a shower and a thought came to me. Maybe Jenny was taking the money. I went into her bag to find her purse.
Her purse was stuffed with loads of notes, flicking the notes there must have been at least a hundred pounds in there. I closed the purse and put in back in her bag. I thought about telling Dad again. Then I thought fuck it, Gill won't believe it, so if I am getting blamed for taking it then I will have some of it.

I know it was wrong, but I took some money out of Jenny's purse. Jenny couldn't say anything because she wasn't supposed to have it.
I was still at college and I had done a year on the English and maths course. It was coming up to choosing another course, so I took an art and design.
I loved it right from the start, but life at home living with Gill was hard. It didn't matter what I did, she just didn't like me.

"Why"

Dad and Gill Got us all together in the lounge. Telling all of us that they were getting married. I felt like I was losing my dad again and was still finding it hard to handle the stuff in my head.

Me and Gill would argue all the time, so for a quite life I kept out of her way it was just like when Alan first moved in .

While I was out with Claire I said, ' I am almost sixteen now I can't take the tension at home anymore, Gill is driving me mad.'

Claire said, ' Well why don't we move out together and rent a room.' I loved the idea and couldn't wait to start looking.

Claire found out that one of our mates was living in a house. So we went round one night and found out that there was a room free.

We rang the landlord and he agreed that we could share the room. I was so happy that evening as I was going to get some breathing space from Gill.

I went home and told Dad what we was planning. He looked sad; I could tell from his voice he didn't like the idea much .

He said 'It was ok - I will help you with all the paperwork and set up what needed doing.'

After a week or so we was given a moving in date; I couldn't wait.

Best of all, it wasn't far from dad, so I could pop round to see him when ever I liked.

"Why"

Chapter Twenty One

It was the day that I was moving out from Dad's house, I was nervous but ready to go. Claire came round early, asking dad if he could help with her stuff as dad had a car; he was happy to help. we all went to the house and Dad stayed for a cup of tea. He had brought us some food and gave me Forty pound, to keep me going until I got my money from the job centre. Dad said his goodbyes and left us too it.

Our room was one of five in the house - we didn't have much in the way of furniture but it did us. Our friend's room was next to ours; the rest of the room had people we didn't know in.

Life at the house was mostly parties. I got talking to Mark, one of the blokes in the house. He was about ten years older than me. He was nice but he was a bit weird. One night while we was all drinking and having fun.

He said, 'Come into my room - I want to chat to you.'

I went in, thinking there wasn't anything to worry about with everyone in the house. We sat on his bed. ' What do you want to chat about? '

He said, 'I like you and I would like you to be my girlfriend.'

I wasn't into him like that, so I told him, 'I would just like to stay friends.' He didn't seemed to like my answer , but he took it. We went back to the front room where everyone was sitting.

"Why"

Claire called me out next, 'What did mark want you for, Marie?' when I told her what he said she laughed. 'In his dreams.'

I liked the freedom living in the house gave me - always popping round to see dad after college, life was pretty good.

I was loving the chance to express myself in my art course. Sally was doing a computer course. We meet up most lunch times.

She was looking for a job and was leaving college when her first year was up.

She had found a job and left college. We still hung out but not as much as I would've liked. We started to drift apart once she had made new friends at work.

I was getting my head round living away from Dad. At night I was still having nightmares though. Claire would give me a cuddle and calm me down.

She would ask me what I was dreaming about to get in such a state. I always told her I couldn't remember.

Once the job centre had sorted out our money, we were getting thirty pounds each every two weeks. The bills were all in with the rent and the job centre paid it straight to the landlord. So all we had to get with our money was food; we lived on mostly sandwiches and noodles and round Dad's for Sunday lunch.

Mark started asking me out again, every time getting the same answer from me. Claire had found herself Andy, a nice fella that drove.

Most nights we would go out, which was nice, because it got me away from Mark.

"Why"

Mark was starting to freak me out, being outside the
bathroom door when I came out. I felt like I was always
being watched all the time.

One night Claire was out with Andy, so I sat up in our
room and done some of my design homework. As I sat
on my bed, the door opened and mark walked in. I
snapped at him, 'What do you think you are doing just
walking in like that.'

He didn't speak; he just walked over to where I was. He
sat on my bed next to me - he was so close he might as
well been sitting on my lap. Without warning he grabbed
my hair and pulled me back on to the bed forcing a kiss
on me. I shouted, 'Get off me.'

He let go of my hair. I got straight off the bed and
pointed to the door ' Get out now, Mark.'

He got up. I thought he was going to leave, but no, he
walked right up to me. Pushing me until I was up against
the wall, he grabbed my jaw and started to kiss me
again.

Looking right into my eyes he said, 'I want you as my
girlfriend and you haven't got a choice.'

The strong smell of alcohol on his breath made me shake
with fear. I was right back being that frightened little girl
Alan controlled. Now I had another monster wanting
me as his toy.

He kissed me again and left the room. As soon as I was
alone, the fear was too much and I was sick everywhere.
After that night he would tell me to go into his room and
stay there until he joined me. I wanted to tell Claire but
he said he would hurt her.

"Why"

Most of the time Clare was out these days. He told everyone else in the house that we was going out with each other. Nearly ever night he would force himself on me kissing and touching me.

The room he had glass doors which lead out to the back garden.

When we was in his room one night he jumped up. ' Did you hear that?'

I said, 'No, I didn't hear anything.'

He said, ' I heard a noise in the garden.' he went out into the garden to have a look.

He came staggering back in with cuts all down his arms and one on his face, his clothes covered in blood.

'what happened out there?' I asked

He said, 'There was someone out there; they slashed me with a knife, they said they was looking for you.'

I panicked, thinking it was Alan's family. I said, 'We should call the police.'

He said, 'Its ok they have gone now, there is no point calling the police.' Looking back now, I know he was playing with my mind to control me. Every night that Claire was out he raped me.

One night he said, 'I want to play a game with you tonight.'

I told him, 'I just want to go back to my room to sleep.' hoping he would leave me alone but that's not my luck.

He ordered me to lay on the bed,.I did it out of fear, I was only there with him out of fear.

He tied my hands and legs to the bed and covered my eyes.

240

"Why"

The flash backs from the dirty houses that Alan used to
take me to running riot in my head.
All I could do was listen and try and work out what he
was going to do. All of a sudden, I felt this pain up my
bottom; at the same time I felt him pushing inside me
and his disgusting lips on my skin.
 He was pushing really hard. He untied my legs and
rolled me over pulling me up onto my knees, he forced
himself into my bum.
 I hated it - the pain was too much. He always made sure
the house was empty or it was late so everyone was
asleep.
I hated him so much but I was scared. I wished I had
never moved in that house. He was being horrible to
Claire so she kept out of his way by going out with her
man all the time. I wish she had noticed her friend was
so scared and needed saving.
Then came her bombshell: Claire said, 'I am moving out.
I have found another room to rent but it.s only a single. I
will still hang out with you but I can't take Mark's
bullying anymore.'
I sat on my bed with my head in my hands as I asked,
'When are you going?'
She said, 'Today, Marie.'
I asked, 'where did you find that room?'
She said, 'One of Andy's mates has a spare room to rent
out'
I didn't blame her but I just wish she had taken me with
her.
I had nowhere else to go - I was stuck in that house with
Mark, not that he would let me leave.

"Why"

Claire didn't take her clothes when she left that day; she said she will pick them up in a few days. Now Clare was out of the way every night he would abuse me in some way or another.

Mark kept saying, 'I hope your not getting any ideas about moving out because you know I wouldn't like that.'

He knew I had no way out of the house and was stuck there with him.

 Mark would use anything he could think of to control me, causing my life to go to rat shit again.

 Two days after Clare left, she popped round to get her stuff. Mark answered the door and let her in.

 As she made her way up the stairs to my room mark said, ' I don't know why you came back for your clothes, you're not having them.'

Claire said, ' What do you mean I am not having them?'

Mark raised his voice. ' I am going to burn your clothes because you owe me rent.'

Claire replied, ' I have paid my rent to the landlord - you don't own this house, my rent has fuck all to do with you.'

Mark hit the roof. ' I run this house - what I say goes and you're not getting your clothes.'

'You're a nobody, Mark,' she screamed at him.

With that Mark ran up the stairs and dragged Claire out on to the street and closed the door.

Everyone in the house stood looking at him not saying a word.

The following evening Claire returned with Andy.

"Why"

Mark had been drinking for most of the day and was just ordering me into his room when they knocked on the door. Mark opened the door and started shouting at them. ' You can both fuck off, you owe me rent.' With that mark pulled a knife out of the back of his trousers and chased them both down the road.

Mark returned a short while later with a case of beer under his arm.

He was in the kitchen when there was a loud bang at the door.

'Get that Marie if, it's Claire tell her I will cut her head off if she steps in this house.'

I opened the door. standing in front of me was eight or nine men with Clare and on the door step another three big blokes. One of the men on the door step started shouting as soon as I opened the door.

I was at breaking point. Freaking out I slammed the door shut and ran in to the kitchen. I could still hear them shouting outside and mark shouting back at them.

I burst into tears and slumped into the corner on the kitchen floor, with my hands over my ears to drown out the shouting.

Over the muffled shouting, I heard a couple of loud thuds. I looked up and the front door burst open and all the men outside came running in.

Mark grabbed the knife off the kitchen work top and ran out into the garden.

All the men that were outside were now standing around me in the kitchen shouting into the garden. I coward in the corner just wanting it all to stop.

"Why"

As loud as I could I kept shouting, ' Stop, stop, stop.' But none of them could hear me over the shouting.

Mark was in the garden waving the knife shouting, ' Come on then, I will do the lot of you,'

Andy said, 'Where are Claire's clothes you prick?'

' I told you she isn't having them now fuck off.' Mark shouted back.

The shouting continued until I heard the faint sound of sirens getting louder.

Most of the men that ran in house left the house as the sirens got closer.

All that were left was Claire, Andy and his mate when the police ran into the house. I picked myself up off the floor. The police officer asked us what was going on. While we was telling him, more police officers arrived. One of the officers gave Andy and his mate a caution, telling them to go or they would be arrested. Claire stayed in the kitchen with me as the police ran out into the garden wrestling Mark to the ground.

As they took him away he looked at me like he was going to kill me.

After all the mayhem had finished Claire said that she would stay with me that night.

"Why"

Chapter Twenty Two

The following morning Andy and his mate came round to pick up Clare's clothes. I went down and put the kettle on for a cup of tea.

Andy's mate joined me in the kitchen. He said,' Are you ok after last night's carry on ?'

I said, 'I am fine thanks.' ' I am sorry, I am simon,I didn't catch your name.'

' I am Marie.'

He nodded and smiled and carried on with the small talk. Just as they was all leaving the house a police car pulled up outside.

Two officers got out and asked if they could come in. Once inside they told me that mark was a metal health patient and was going to be locked up in a secure mental health unit.

As they left I closed the door, leaning on it thinking why me.

Simon came round the next day saying, 'Claire asked me to come round and make sure you're ok.'

I chuckled. ' Tell her I am fine.'

An awkward silence filled the kitchen. Simon took a deep breath.

'Erm, I was wondering would you like to go for a drink some time?'

Unsure what he was after I replied, ' I don't know you at all.'

He said, 'Well get to know me then you might like what you find.'

"Why"

Still wary about him I said, 'I will think about it.'
He smiled and said, 'I will take that answer.'
Everyday that week simon popped round just to see if I
was ok, occasionally asking if I had made my mind up
about going for a drink.
 I kept saying I didn't know him well enough, but I was
warming to him slowly.
He came up with the idea of going out in a foursome
with Claire and Andy.
I panicked - how could I say no now if Claire was going
to be there so I agreed to go.
Simon called round for me and walked me to the pub.
All the way there I was nervous and thinking if Claire
isn't there then I was coming home.
As we approached the pub, Claire and Andy were
standing outside making me relax a bit.
Simon treated me like a princess and made me feel
special that night.
 While he was walking me home that night I agreed that
just the two of us should go out for a drink. On the
Monday morning at college I bumped into Claire. She
said, ' I will meet you after college and come back to
yours - I want to hear what you think about Simon.'
I laughed. ' There is nothing to tell.'
Claire said, ' Yeah right, I am still meeting you..'
College finished and as promised Clare was at the gate
waiting for me.
 As we walked home she wanted all the gossip but there
was none to tell.
We got back to my house. A letter had been slid under
my door.

"Why"

It was from my landlord, saying that because of all the trouble we all had to leave the house in five days,as he was selling it.

I said, ' For fuck sake, what next.'

Claire asked, 'What is up Marie?'

I handed her the letter. ' Read that.'

We carried on talking, the contents of the letter not sinking in.

After a cup of tea Claire left, leaving me with the problem of where I was going to live. I didn't have a clue what I was going to do.

Within an hour I got a visit from Claire and simon. We went into the kitchen and made some tea. I was a nervous wreck; my hands were shaking as I was pouring out the water.

Simon said, 'I am sorry to hear that you are being kicked out because of all the trouble.'

I said, 'Its not your fault.'

Claire asked, 'What are you going to do?'

I said, 'I don't know, I can't go back to Dad's because I don't get on with Gill, so I am stuffed really.'

Claire put her arms around me and said, 'Don't worry, I will help you find something.'

Simon said, 'If you don't mind sleeping on the sofa, you could come and sleep at my place.'

I looked at him over Claire's shoulder. I wasn't sure what to say to his offer.

Before I could answer Claire let go of me and said, 'That's a great idea. I am in his spare room.'

Simon said, ' How long before you have to be out of here?'

"Why"

I said, 'I have got to be out in five days.'
He said, 'Well think about it, the offer will still be there if you need it.'
I thought about it while we drank our tea.
Simon said, ' I have got to go now, I have an early start in the morning, but don't forget the offer is there if you need it,'
I said, 'Well I have five days to leave, so if I can't find anything id love to take you up on your offer.'
He smiled. 'Ok you have got my number, so just let me know.'
I said, 'I will thanks.'
When they left, I went up into my room feeling empty and numb.
I just couldn't believe that my life just seemed to always go wrong.
That night I laid awake thinking about Simon's offer.
After milling it over in my head, I couldn't see any other way out of my predicament.
 Maybe it would be ok, as Claire was living there.
So I rang simon the next day to take him up on his offer, he was happy that I was going to be moving in at his place. Up until then he kept popping round and ringing me, checking if I needed anything or just to make sure I was ok.
He had a really caring voice, I didn't get any bad vibes when I spoke to him or when I was in his company, but I still had my guard up.
On the day I moved in he took a day off work just to help me move - in a nutshell he couldn't do enough for me.

"Why"

Claire was always there which made me feel safe and the more time I spent with him the more I liked him.

I had been living at Simon's for about for about four weeks, when I was walking home from college. I noticed a car that was following me; I was almost home when it disappeared.

I got in and closed the front door behind me. Something snapped inside my head. I couldn't take this living in fear anymore. I ran into the bathroom and locked the door.

I took Simon's razor out of the cupboard and sat on the edge of the bath.

Talking to my Nan: 'I am coming to be with you, Nan because everyone wants to hurt me down here, I don't want to hurt anymore or be scared for my life.'

I didn't even hear the front door go as I started to lash into my arms.

Someone was knocking on the bathroom door. I shouted at them to go away. It was Simon's voice on the other side of the door. He said, 'Marie, are you OK, you sound upset again.'

I said, 'Please leave me alone Simon.'

He said, ' Open the door. I am worried about you, please opened the door and maybe we can talk.' I didn't take any notice.

With him pleading with me, I just shut off and watched the blood trickle down my arms from the slashes.

Simon trying the door handle to get the door open, while I was in a frenzy slashing at my arms.

I started to feel dizzy, sliding down on to the floor.

"Why"

My eyes were closing as I saw simon come smashing through the door, then it all faded into darkness .
I woke up in hospital. I looked down at my arms bandaged up.
Lying my head back on the pillow, I said, 'Fuck it, I am still here.'
A voice said, 'Nurse, nurse.'
Turning my head in the direction of the voice, To see simon sitting at my bedside. I asked him, 'What are you doing here?'
He said, 'Making sure you're OK. I am not leaving you until you are.'
I fell back to sleep, when I woke up simon was gone.
A nurse came over and said, 'Don't worry, he has only gone to get a coffee, he will be back soon.'
I asked, 'How long has he been here?'
She said, ' He has been in every visiting time since you came in.' I didn't know what to make of her answer.
A Doctor said, 'Your arms aren't as bad as they looked, but I want you to stay in hospital until I am happy they are healing well, I would like you to talk to a head doctor as well .' but I wasn't having any of that.
Two weeks passed before I was allowed to go home.
Simon picked me up from hospital and took me home.
He gave up his bed and slept on the sofa - again he couldn't do enough for me.
That weekend he bought a pizza and a bottle of wine and said, 'Right, me and you are going to talk.'
As the wine flowed he asked, 'Why do you want to die?'

"Why"

I said, 'Because the world is full of nasty people that just wanted to control me and hurt me.'

He looked into my eyes and said, 'Oh Marie not everyone wants to hurt you, I want to look after you, I would like to be with you your a lovely girl and really pretty - would you consider being my girlfriend?'

I freaked out. I got up, and started shouting, 'What so you can control me and rape me.'

He looked at me with shock on his face. I fell into a heap on the floor. Simon came over to me and said, 'I would never hurt you and if you're my girl no one will ever hurt you again.'

I looked up to see his face. He went to give me a kiss; his lips felt good.

I pulled away saying, 'I am dirty - why would you want me I am too damaged.' Simon said, 'Because I can see you are a lovely person.'

After that evening we spent lots of time together. I started to trust him.

At last I had a decent man in my life. He treated me like a princess and respected me - I wasn't his slave or his toy to control.

Life was getting better and better. Simon made me see life was worth living.

We had been together for about nine months, when I started to be sick all the time. I had fallen pregnant. I was over the moon but scared at the same time. I wasn't sure how simon was going to react to the news as we hadn't been seeing each other long. I couldn't wait for him to get home from work and tell him my news.

"Why"

The day dragged. The nearer it got to him coming home
the knot in my stomach got tighter. As soon as he was in
the door I told him. He grabbed me spinning me round
and said, 'That's great news, I will get changed and we
can go tell my mum and dad and your dad.'
Later that year I gave birth to a little boy. As he was
placed in my arms I looked up and said, 'Thanks, Nan for
not coming to get me. I couldn't be happier you was
right: I won in the end.'

20448609R00150

Printed in Great Britain
by Amazon